More Praise for *The Power of Networking*

"During my career I have interacted with innumerable business professionals. Sheila Savar made a lasting impression on me, because her demeanor is natural and genuine. She demonstrates that the art of being a powerful networker is just being yourself."
– *John Derrick, Retired Chairman and CEO, Pepco Holdings*

"Sheila Savar's latest book provides valuable insight and information about the increasingly important subject of networking."
– *Alan A. Malinchak, Chief Learning Officer,*
ManTech International Corporation

"This book is an eye opener for those who focus on efficiency and return on investment. It provides no-nonsense coverage of what it takes to build positive relationships that are essential for getting new business."
– *Dev Raheja, President, Design for Competitiveness, Inc.*
and author, Assurance Technologies Principles And Practices
and Zen and the Art of Breakthrough Quality Management

"Finally! A how-to guide on NETWORKING that offers the novice and experienced professional a blueprint for how to achieve personal and professional success. Sheila Savar's common sense approach acknowledges the realities of time and budget constraints, and individual styles and differing goals. Make room on the bookshelf, because building a powerful NETWORK of contacts *is a must for serious-minded professionals,* and owning this book is the first step in showing you how!"
– *Eileen McCaffrey, Executive Director, Orphan Foundation of America*

"Sheila Savar's focused and hands-on strategic approach in her book helped me to prioritize my networking investment in time, money and energy. Consequently, I cancelled four low-return events and will instead invest in an all Senior Executive level conference. That is how her book helped me add value to my business and to me personally."
– Maria Velez de Berliner, President, Latin Intelligence Corporation

"Success in networking doesn't just happen. You must set goals, create strategies and implement relationship-centric processes that get you noticed quickly. Power networkers know the secrets of building successful networks and so will you after reading this book. It's a must read for every person serious about their career and business success!"
– Angela Drummond, CEO, SiloSmashers and Collaborations

"I purchased and read your book, **The Power of Networking**. I found your networking guide extremely helpful. It is written in a format that flows and is easy to understand so that the skills can be comprehended and applied instantaneously. You have outlined a networking process and strategy that will help me approach networking with the right frame of mind, intention, and focus to achieve desired goals. Well done! The other sections, such as the proper way to dress and interact with a person during the actual networking process were inspiring. They will take my network skills to the next level. And yes, I am one of those people that has too many business cards to count. Your advice on specific technology networking programs that organize contacts is invaluable. I could go on and on how about how this book is going to help me. Thanks for the knowledge. It is a privilege to be in your network!"
– Dan Grapin

"Sheila, I got my copy of your book and started reading it. I find it has so many helpful networking hints I had not thought of before....this is especially true on the volunteer aspect. The suggestions I've gotten from that point alone has made the book worthwhile, although I can't wait to pick up more tips as I complete it. Thank you for your insight and for phrasing it in easily understood and grasped language. Take care and best wishes for your continued success."
– Gene D. Smith, PMP

THE POWER OF NETWORKING

A How-To Networking Guide for Your Career & Business Success!

To Konstantin

warm wishes,

Sheil Savar

THE POWER OF NETWORKING

A How-To Networking Guide for Your Career & Business Success!

BAMA PRESS

Reston, Virginia

www.savar.biz

THE POWER OF NETWORKING:
A How-To Networking Guide for Your Career & Business Success!
by Sheila Savar

Published by BAMA Press
1900 Campus Commons Drive, Suite 100, Reston, VA 20191
www.savar.biz

Cover and design by Sagetopia, LLC
Cover photograph by Tony Awad

Publishers' Cataloging-in-Publication
(Provided by Quality Books, Inc.)

Savar, Sheila.
    The power of networking : a how-to networking guide
for your career & business success! / [Sheila Savar].
    p. cm.
    Includes index.
    LCCN 2007905420
    ISBN-13: 978-0-9798533-0-2
    ISBN-10: 0-9798533-0-3

    1. Business networks. 2. Success in business.
I. Title.

HD69.S8S28 2008   650.1'3
                           QBI07-600241

Dedication

This book is dedicated to my parents. To my father, the finest and most refined diplomat ever! Thank you for exposing me to all those embassy parties during my growing up years. They provided the perfect training ground for developing and refining my interpersonal and networking skills. It was you who taught me the importance of making great first and lasting impressions, following political and business protocols, and most importantly being a gracious host and caring humanitarian who treats everyone with respect and dignity. Every cardinal, every blue jay, every flower I see reminds me of you.

And to my mother, who through genetics and example passed on to me the gifts of warmth, authenticity, gab (or great communication skills) and a generous heart always wanting to help others. Your charm, sunny disposition and great sense of humor attract people to you. I'd like to think I possess those qualities through inheritance from you! Thank you for always being my #1 fan and believing in and supporting my dreams and efforts.

Acknowledgments

Writing a book is a solitary experience, but creating it is definitely a group effort. I have many people to thank. Dave Gerber, a business contact referred me to his editor and now mine Gaye Newton of Galibren Written Treasures.

In addition to editing this book, Gaye provided me with valuable information that simplified and expedited the publishing process. It would have been much more difficult and time-consuming without her expertise and generosity. She also referred me to Sagetopia, a company that designed her own book cover and layout, assuring me that they were artists as well as experts. She was right! Thank you, Sagetopia for a job well done. A very special thank you to Gaye Newton for all the help you provided me in addition to the great job you did as my editor!

Heartfelt thanks go to my publicist, Monika Taylor, a principal of Three Way Communiqué. Monika and I met through the United Way. She is a special friend as well as a talented businesswoman, and I feel very fortunate to have her on my team. Thank you, Monika! My thanks also extend to my friend and mentor Dev Raheja, a fellow author and consultant, for his support, encouragement and wisdom. I value our friendship.

Proofreading a manuscript is a necessary yet painstaking endeavor. Well deserved thanks go to my mother, my cousin Margaret Wright and my dear friends Evelyn Godwin and Roxanne Alston-Tart.

Finally and most importantly, I'd like to thank my mother, sisters and brothers for the support and encouragement they have shown me throughout this project's undertaking. It's so much easier to attempt something new if those closest to you are supportive. I can't express how much your support meant to me. I hope I have been there for you as well.

I wrote this book not just to teach how to network but also to demonstrate how instrumental a strong network is in helping you achieve your personal and professional goals. Whether your objective is to acquire sales, grow your business, find a new job, enter or re-enter the workforce, plan a career change, find a mentor, alliance-partner, medical specialist, a suburb hairstylist or even a day-care center, you can achieve whatever you desire more productively and efficiently if you have a strong network to help you (and you them). Following my presentations, numerous audience members consistently approach me to share with me their restored energy and renewed determination to pursue their objectives using the networking information I provided. I hope that after reading this book, you too will share their feelings.

Audience members that touch me most deeply and hold a very special place in my heart are the university students in the Orphan Foundation of America's (OFA) summer internship program. These young people are former Foster children. OFA's mission is to provide former Foster children with university and trade school scholarships, mentoring support, internship placement, student care packages and a host of other services that these students need to ensure they graduate and have a chance at a brighter successful future. I am a strong supporter, friend and admirer of OFA and its Executive Director, Eileen McCaffrey. To those summer interns that I've met and trained, I want you to know that I am so proud of you for your courage and determination to have a better life. I treasure the notes you send me after every presentation, and you are often in my thoughts. There is no doubt that you will succeed. This book is my gift to help you achieve that success.

All the people I've mentioned, both business and personal connections, are a part of my vast network of contacts. It is because of many of them that I was able to write and publish this book in just four months. That's the power of *my* network in action. Now, let's get started creating *yours*!

Table of Contents

PART I

The Value of Networking

Chapter 1

Networking: Basics and Beyond

Who do you know?

You've met thousands of people in your lifetime. You've come to know many of them, while others have made only brief, random appearances, never to be seen again. What if one of those random people walked away with what could have been a great business opportunity for you? What if you had information that could have helped that person's small business save him a significant amount of money? You both could have benefited from a little networking.

If you list everyone you know right now—family members, friends, business associates and contacts, neighbors, your plumber, the real estate agent who sold you your house 10 years ago, people in your schools and places of worship and clubs, even that guy from down the street who mows his lawn too early on Sundays—you will have in your hands your current network.

That's a network? On the most basic level, yes. A network is a collection, so to speak, of all the people you know. Some will have more significant roles in your life than others, but they're all included. And when you meet new people, they're included, too.

NETWORKING BASICS

Networking, the act of creating and managing your network, is something everyone does to some degree, even children. A girl building a sandcastle on the beach isn't content with her design and needs a larger container to form a tower. Her friend knows another child a few yards away who has the perfect bucket. The friend arranges a loan of the bucket, and the castle is a masterpiece. Your neighbor needs an attorney. Your hairdresser's son is the best in the area, so you make the connection. You're using personal contacts in your network to help others and vice versa. That's basic networking.

While that works well for casual situations, effective networking in the business world is much more focused and formal. Most people don't keep an organized list of everyone they run across or have a process that keeps them on task bringing the right people into their networks. But if you want to put networking to work for you, that's precisely what you need to do.

So who are those "right" people you need to meet? That depends on what you want to accomplish. When you have a goal—starting or growing your business, getting a new job, changing your career— you need a way to locate resources quickly and efficiently. You need to know which people to call on for the assistance you need. Where do you find them?

Well, who do you know?

Unless you've spent your life in a cave or on a remote island, you already have a network. But what shape is it in? Does it include people capable of helping you achieve your goals? Are you in a position to help them? Do you have a plan to put yourself in places where you can meet and interact with these people?

NETWORKING BEYOND THE BASICS

True networking is the most efficient, productive and ultimately most cost-effective method of getting in front of decision makers who can open doors to sales and career opportunities and close business deals. Continuous networking increases sales, referrals and your customer base. It promotes you, your company name and brand in the community. It also helps you find an influential mentor, land your dream job, gain access to venture capital funds, jump start your career, help you avoid costly or time-consuming mistakes, even find the best day care providers and doctors.

Successful business people network because they understand that face-to-face meetings and relationship building is by far the most effective method of gaining appointments and closing sales with key decision makers. What's "relationship" got to do with business? Everything! It may be business, but we are people first. And people prefer to buy from people they know and like.

IN THIS BOOK

Most people that attend my networking presentations, and even you who have purchased this book, probably did so to learn how to network better. You may have no previous networking experience, or you are an entrepreneur or corporate employee responsible for revenue generation and know you must attend networking functions to get business. But you really dread these events, partly because you are not a "people person" and partly because you are not sure how to go about networking. This book covers three important aspects of networking: strategy, process, and support methodology.

Strategy: Networking without a strategy is like attempting to travel to a new city without a map. You may never get there, but should you somehow manage to arrive, it will have taken you much longer and cost you much more. We're going to begin by learning how to create your networking strategy based on your unique goals and objectives.

Process: You will learn *how* to network using an eight-step process that takes you from preparing for an event to the moment you leave. If you apply these steps consistently, you can become an exceptional networker.

Methodology: Being an exceptional networker alone doesn't guarantee you business or career success. In addition to developing relationships with those key contacts you make (those that can positively impact your goals and objectives), you must also have a methodology for building and staying connected to all your contacts, otherwise you'll forget them. And they'll forget you. Technology plays an important role here. We'll discuss creating systems, including online resources that keep contact information at your fingertips.

I have also included some newly defined business concepts that more accurately reflect the nature of business relationships formed through effective networking and a list of resources that can support your networking efforts.

This book is designed to be user-friendly and easy to read. Once you've read it, please use it often as a resource guide for your successful networking. Reading it once will not help you transfer information into application. I suggest you keep it handy (like in your car), so you can use it as a quick reference guide just before going into a networking function. It will be a confidence booster!

WHO SHOULD READ THIS BOOK

Obviously businesspeople will reap many benefits from increased networking skills. But this book is not only for people tasked with revenue generation. While the primary reason most people network is to secure business, there are many secondary, valuable reasons for creating a large network of contacts. You see, in networking situations you are dealing with people, and *it's all about relationships*. If people like you, they'll help you, period! Okay, exclamation point.

Entrepreneurs and Small Business Owners: Entrepreneurs are often proficient in certain areas (e.g., IT, accounting or graphic design) and decide to start their own businesses based on those skills. If this is you, your strength lies in the *work* you perform—your specific skills—prior to going solo. Most likely you were not responsible for revenue generation before. Well, you are now!

You must become responsible for finding new business. The first step is prospecting (looking for new business). One of the best prospecting methods is networking. Many entrepreneurs, being task- rather than social-oriented, dread the idea of networking, prospecting and selling. But there's good news! If you are a task-oriented person, you are logically oriented and can appreciate the strategy and process behind networking that this little book provides. By following these recommendations, you can become a successful networker. Your task orientation may never allow you to become the Tiger Woods of networking, but the point is to get the business—and those wonderful referrals—you need to be successful.

Recent College Graduates: You may be thinking, "I certainly don't need to know this, right?" Wrong! You need to start building your network today. It can help you get your first job. Positions posted in the paper and on the Internet are the leftover jobs, the ones that couldn't be filled by people in an employer's network. Using your networking skills and attending networking functions allows you to land that great first job, find valuable mentors, and in the future, change career paths or find good employees. So don't hesitate. Begin building your powerful network now.

The Unemployed and Career Changers: Fired, laid off or just hate your job? You can play the victim and obsess over your problem, or you can become an empowered person and take charge of *your* life! How? The best place to begin is by reaching out to your network. If that doesn't work, then go where your future employers go: to networking events. If someone has a great job opening, who do you think has the better chance of getting the interview, the person he or she meets at a network function and who expresses an interest in the job, or a stranger who sends a resume? Believe me, assuming you're both qualified, the answer is almost always the person he or she met.

If you're switching careers, trying to get a stranger to accept or embrace your job transition by reading your resume is almost futile. But suppose you attend a networking event where relevant decision makers go, and you meet the CEO of a small or mid-sized company. He can see that your unique combination of intelligence, charm, and vivacious personality, coupled with your experience in your previous career, might make you an excellent candidate for a position in your desired field. He invites you to interview. That would never have happened with a resume alone.

Corporate Employees: A company is like a shark; it has to keep moving or it dies. Each year a company's earnings must exceed its previous year's, or there is no growth. Every employee should understand that the majority of that growth depends on him or her; that he or she is either contributing to the customer experience (earning client loyalty) or contaminating it (causing client attrition). Long term, only *client loyalty* leads to corporate growth.

If you play a role in your company's revenue generation goals, networking is vital to attracting new business, meeting other corporate decision-makers, staying abreast of the business community, being a spokesperson for your company, spreading awareness about your products and services and representing them in a manner that demonstrates the corporate brand. Even if you do not generate revenue, it's also a great way to make a name for yourself and become a power person in your business community.

Information is power. The stronger and larger your business and personal network, the more value it provides you and others, because it gives you access to valuable information. A well-balanced network makes you a notable resource in the business community and transforms you into a person of influence—a *power person!*

Chapter 2
Business Definitions for the New Millennium

We are well into the new millennium, yet we continue to use what I consider outdated business and sales terminology to identify and classify companies and people. We no longer conduct business the way we did fifty, thirty or even ten years ago. Why are we still using outdated terms and labels that often discount or devalue the seller? We need to use terminology that equalizes and more accurately reflects the interdependence between buyers and sellers today.

I feel strongly about the power of words. They can define, categorize, identify, judge, label, limit and more. Some business phrases have always been, in my opinion, inappropriate and sometimes even offensive. So I am introducing new millennium word choices that I consider more appropriate in today's business climate. If you agree with me, please replace the outdated, old school phrases.

OLD SCHOOL: DELETE "ELEVATOR PITCH"

"Elevator Pitch" has always made me cringe. It sounds insincere and lacks substance. I imagine some poor sales representative finding himself in the fortunate (or unfortunate) position of being in an elevator with an executive he wanted to meet. He only has a few seconds until the elevator stops, so he must rush through his pitch and hope that the executive is listening and sufficiently impressed to give him an appointment. Doesn't this sound degrading to you?

Pitching (monologue) rather than *conversing* (dialogue) puts the salesperson in an inferior position and sets the stage for a negative relationship with this decision-maker. Let's also examine the word "pitch." Imagine a pitcher throwing a baseball to a batter. His goal is to strike the batter out. This is an old school, win-lose mentality and no way to conduct business in today's sophisticated climate. There is no such thing as win-lose selling; there is only win-win and lose-lose.

People buy from people they like and trust; it's all about the relationship. When people need something, they are more likely to ask someone in their network for a referral than to go to complete strangers. The salesperson in the elevator is not only a complete stranger, he lacks authenticity.

You may be shaking your head and saying, "Sheila, you're taking this too literally. It does not have to take place in an elevator. It's just about pitching the message in a short amount of time to the right executive." It doesn't matter. Its human nature to run when chased. When you pitch anything, it's one-sided and excludes the other person from participation. There is only a monologue—no dialogue—so no opportunity for relationship building. You will, in the mind of the decision-maker, be trying to *sell* him and whereas people love to buy, they hate to be sold! To him, you're just another vendor. We'll talk about that word shortly.

NEW MILLENNIUM: REPLACE WITH "COMPANY POSITION STATEMENT"

A Company Position Statement is a strategic message about your company, its purpose and its targeted market. It lasts 15 to 20 seconds and should be brief enough to gain the listeners' interest and encourage them to ask questions. This creates a *dialogue* (new millennium) instead of a *monologue* (old school). Remember, dialogues engage people and allow relationship building.

Have you attended networking events and asked people what they do, only to fail to understand a single thing they said? Do you ask for clarification? If you're like most people, you may be too shy to ask, or you don't want to appear ignorant. The sad truth is that many people create complicated Company Position Statements with fancy verbiage that does more harm than good. Most people will not understand it, and they will not ask for clarification. This is a lost opportunity to establish a dialogue and build relationships and business opportunities. So keep it simple and clear. We'll have more on this in Part III.

OLD SCHOOL: DELETE "VENDOR"

I find this term demeaning when referring to business *provider-partners*. To me, a *vendor* is a company that provides little or no value to your customers' experience. Their products and services (e.g., filtered water, coffee, cleaning supplies and services, paper towels, etc.) are useful to your internal organization, but they do not earn loyalty from your clients. Vendors are easily replaceable. Exceptional provider-partners are not.

NEW MILLENNIUM: REPLACE WITH "BUSINESS PROVIDER-PARTNERS"

Your business provider-partners help you provide your clients with exceptional customer experiences that earn client loyalty, expand your business opportunity and increase your bottom-line profitability. But business provider-partners are still being called vendors, even though they bear little resemblance to the above definition. There are several major differences between the two. Provider-partners:

- Are very educated and are experts in their fields.

- Help you look good (or bad) to your clients.

- Help you earn (or lose) client loyalty.

- Can make or break the customer experience and either help you grow or cost you your customers.

- Often call on your prospective clients, so they are in a position to provide you with referrals and leads.

- May need your services at a future date, such that you become the provider-partner and they become the client.

For the reasons mentioned above, choose your provider-partners carefully. Treat them well. They know people, and they can either bring you business or keep it from you.

Does that mean that the respect and courtesy you accord an individual should be based on the value they bring to you and your organization? Absolutely not! As you build your powerful network, you want to be known as an extraordinary person who treats everyone like a CEO, regardless of their status or position. Good and bad manners precede us. Your good manners are part of your professional brand and help get you recognized as an extraordinary person as well as a power networker. We all want to work with those who treat us well.

How many of you are guilty of failing to return calls, answer e-mails, respond to your provider-partner's proposals, or pay their invoices on time? Have you treated the provider-partner poorly and disrespectfully by keeping him or her waiting when you've scheduled a meeting, taken a call during a meeting or been rude or offensive? This is unacceptable both for you and those who do business with you.

All people are deserving of respect and courtesy. But it's especially foolish to mistreat anyone, vendor or provider-partner. They are selling to your competitors and clients. Don't think they won't talk when they've been mistreated. You could be doing real harm to yourself and your company: not to mention that it is ill-advised to be intentionally rude to anyone.

If a great referral opportunity presents itself to your provider-partner, who do you think will get the referral?

EXAMPLES OF BUSINESS PROVIDER-PARTNERS AND THEIR VALUE TO THE SUCCESS OF YOUR ORGANIZATION

Your Marketing Firm or Graphic Designer: This provider-partner helps create your corporate image by designing your corporate brand and identity. They usually create and develop your business collateral, including your most important one: the business card.

Your business card is seen the most—more than your website or brochures. For that reason alone, your design firm enhances the customer experience. That *adds value* and qualifies the firm as a business provider-partner.

Your Systems Architectural Firm: If a technology company rede-signed your existing computer and network system, streamlined your processes, improved efficiency and systems' compatibility, and enabled management to gain access to time-sensitive reports, they helped you create exceptional customer experiences for your clients. Their efforts, combined with yours, results in your clients' loyalty, expanded business opportunity and increased bottom-line profitability.

Your Consulting and Training Firm: These professionals train your employees to increase product knowledge, performance, quality, productivity and efficiency. Success in business depends primarily on the relationship between your employees and your clients. The better trained your employees, the better the customer experience. Ultimately it's those exceptional experiences provided by your employees that earn client loyalty. The result is new business opportunity, account expansion and client retention. Can you see how an exceptional provider-partner is critical to your business success?

On the flip side, provider-partners that perform poorly, lack good communication skills, fail to respond to requests in a timely manner or do not honor their commitments are detrimental to your organization and your customers. As most human resources professionals will tell you: be slow to hire and quick to fire or it can ruin your business. The same rule applies here. Fire them as quickly as possible before they destroy your customers' experience with your company and endanger your reputation.

Can you now differentiate between a vendor and a provider-partner? Do you understand the critical role your provider-partners play in client acquisition, expansion and retention?

I hope I have convinced you to begin using new millennium terminology, as that is where we now are. Please remember to treat all people well. It is a sign of integrity and says more about you than about the other person. And you never know where the lower level employees of today will be tomorrow. If you treat them well, they'll never forget that, and you'll always have special privileges and treatment. If you treat them poorly, they'll never forget that, either.

How do you want to be branded? What image do you want for your company? Do you want to be considered extraordinary, exemplifying courtesy, respect and integrity? If so, it must be displayed in all of your own and your employees' actions. It must be reflected in your company's brand and brand promise. Make the two congruent as you begin your networking strategy and process. Treat people with respect and courtesy. Display honesty and integrity and a superior work ethic, and your business is almost guaranteed its success!

Part II:

Defining
Your Network

Chapter 3
Part Art, Part Science

As I explained in the Introduction, a network is comprised of all the contacts you have made over the years, be it personal, educational or professional. I consider networking and the act of managing that network, to be both an art and a science.

The art of networking focuses on soft skills, such as verbal and visual communication, relationship building, and understanding the importance of branding a professional image. All these help to create what is uniquely you. It helps you to be noticed and remembered quickly—in a positive way.

Statistics say it takes the average person seven times to be remembered. That's a lot of networking functions to attend just to be noticed! The art of networking reduces the odds in your favor. But first you must have a strategy and a process to ensure your networking success. That's where the science comes in. Science is based on logic and facts. To get the most of your networking experience, you need to develop a *networking strategy* and follow a *tactical process*.

Now here's where things get interesting. I consider strategy to be all science. You determine goals, how to present your business, and what venues you believe will yield the best results. But process is a bit of both science and art. Its science because of the tactical steps you deliberately plan and practice, and its art because of the communication skills you rely on to make it all work. Confused? I'll explain in more detail in Chapter 8.

In most major cities there are literally hundreds of networking functions happening every day. Attending the wrong ones will be very costly, time-consuming, frustrating and demoralizing. And you won't be any closer to the prospects you seek. So before you learn about the art of networking, you first need to create your strategy—your personalized road map designed to help you achieve your networking objectives in the most efficient and productive manner. A strategy will strengthen the quality and results of your networking success by identifying the right organizations, venues, and non-profits that are best suited for the types of decision makers you want to meet. Strategy is covered in Part III.

Based on your strategy, you then develop a tactical networking process. In Part IV, I have provided a step-by-step guide that will show you how to network effectively at an actual event—what to wear and how to act to make favorable first impressions that get you remembered, how to communicate effectively to quickly identify great prospects, and how to include and stay connected with everyone you meet (not just the "right" prospects). Once in front of the key decision makers, you will be able to apply communication and personalized branding skills to differentiate you and leave a lasting, favorable impression.

WHO BELONGS IN YOUR NETWORK?

Though people in business carry different levels of value and importance, everyone you meet should be a part of your network. I said it earlier: Treat everyone you meet like a CEO!

Everyone is worthy and deserving of respect and courtesy. And you never know how or when a person can play an important role in your personal or professional life. It all boils down to how you treated them before they hit the big time. At the very least, in addition to your business contacts, your well-rounded network should include medical professionals, attorneys, insurance and real estate agents, police and firefighters, day care centers, and schools. The more well-rounded your network, the more value it has and the more valuable you become. In short, you become a power person.

Don't forget that you get what you give, so always be willing and ready to first help others achieve their business success. View the business world as abundant, not lacking. There's enough out there for everyone to make money. It's not a matter of getting a small piece of the pie; it's a matter of baking a bigger pie. Help others and you'll be rewarded exponentially.

WHAT CAN NETWORKING DO FOR YOU?

Networking can help you get everything and anything you need more efficiently and productively and in less time and money. A strategically designed network jump starts your business or career success by helping you avoid pitfalls. It quickly identifies and connects you to people who can help you—business alliances, partners, buyers, virtual sales team members, venture capitalists and mentors. It will even help you find or change jobs, if that's your goal.

At any age (but especially when you're in your twenties and thirties), you should use your network to find a mentor with the experience to help you advance personally and professionally. People with mentors achieve success more rapidly and easily. When I was in my twenties and thirties, it certainly would have made things easier if I had heard about mentoring and networking.

Information is power, and a well-connected person is a powerful person. That's the power of your network!

Part II Highlights

- A network is comprised of all the contacts you have made over the years, be it personal, educational or professional.

- Who belongs in your network? Everyone! Because everyone has value to offer to you and you to them. As you build your network, consider the people you want included in addition to prospects and business opportunities. These can range from a great hair stylist (who helps create your professional brand) to insurance and real estate agents to healthcare providers and more. The interesting thing is that you are as likely to learn about a business opportunity or be given a lead through these sources as you are through traditional business sources.

- Networking creates access to all kinds of people with various levels of valuable skills and information. This knowledge will not only help you, you can use it to help others and build a reputation for it.

- The best way to ask for a referral is to give one first.

- *Information is power, and a well-connected person is a powerful and successful person!*

Part III:

Your Networking Strategy

Chapter 4
Identify Your Business or Career Status

Before you can create your networking strategy, you must first identify your current business or career status. Are you a recent college graduate, unemployed, in sales or an entrepreneur? Defining your business status enables you to create the appropriate strategy and select networking venues that meet your business objectives.

Are you wondering why you need to have a strategy for networking? Maybe you aren't sure what a strategy even is.

Your networking strategy is your road map—your guide for moving from point A to point B. It helps you to identify your goals and objectives and creates an action plan that makes you work smarter, not harder. The better your strategy, the less effort you need to expend to get greater results. It helps you to work less and make more!

If you live in a major or mid-sized city, there are literally hundreds of networking functions being held each week. Without a well-defined strategy, you can spend all of your time and money attending various functions and never accomplish your objectives.

What is your current business status?

RECENT COLLEGE GRADUATES, UNEMPLOYED AND JOB SEEKERS

Select venues where you are most likely to meet people capable of helping you or directing you to the right decision makers. A warm, person-to-person introduction always improves your chance of getting an interview compared to responding to an ad. So what networking events should you attend? As you plan your strategy consider these questions:

- What is my occupation?

- Who are the best employers in my field? Do an online search on "Training Magazine," "DiversityBusiness.com" or "Best Companies to Work For" for information on companies.

- What companies interest me? Research them. Remember, the cultural environment is as important as the job. If you are a casual person, working in a formal business environment will make you miserable and won't endear you to your colleagues either.

- What is the vertical market of my occupation? Vertical means the industry. If you are a graphic designer, for example, your occupation is considered to be part of the marketing industry. If you are a network administrator, you are in the IT or technology industry.

You want to attend networking functions in your industry (vertical), because people there are often privy to job openings. The actual decision makers might be there too. I know of several people that moved into town and had jobs within three months just by attending the right networking functions. Does three months sound long? Consider this: my cousin, a corporate attorney who moved to the Washington, D.C. area, was told by a recruiter that there were no positions currently available in her field in our town. If she had listened to him instead of trusting her instincts and attending a networking function, she would not have met the woman who offered her a great job as a corporate attorney!

- You may also want to attend networking events by horizontal market. An example of a horizontal market is all companies with less than 100 employees or with annual revenues under $10,000,000. These are companies in several industries (IT, telecom, construction, etc.) that employ people in your field.

- Check your local newspapers, business journals and online sources for weekly calendars of events and job fair postings.

STARTUPS AND ENTREPRENEURS

You need a different networking strategy. Starting with the end in mind, what are your networking objectives? These should be among yours:

- Find prospects
- Find teaming partners and business alliances
- Build a virtual sales team
- Identify provider-partners
- Find mentors
- Get referrals

Go to networking functions where you will meet those people. For example, to find teaming partners and business alliances, attend your industry associations or organizations. You may even get some business from industry members.

When you're looking for prospects, *go where your prospects go.* A corporate attorney and rainmaker should attend not only the local Bar Association events, but events where prospective clients are most likely to attend. So first identify the types of clients and the level of people you want to meet. Then identify the associations and organizations that cater to those people. For example, a technology company that wants to create a niche market specializing in the financial sector should attend conferences and networking events sponsored by financial associations such as the Mortgage Bankers Association.

CORPORATE EMPLOYEES

In all the years I worked in the corporate sector, I was never aware of networking or the influence it had on one's career. It wasn't until I was a senior vice president of a technology company six years ago that I learned about networking through my local chamber. A year later, when I was ready to start Savar & Associates, it was the chamber that helped get me into their incubator program.

If you're an entry- or mid-level corporate employee, attend networking functions to:

- Promote your company (PR is everyone's responsibility!).

- Find prospects (again everyone's responsibility).

- Expand your circle of contacts to include mentors, career advancement and change professionals, day care providers, support groups, women's groups or just about anything of value to you.

- Get involved with non-profits and community service organizations. Not only is serving your community a worthwhile cause, you will probably meet more senior executives through your involvement than through any other means. The contacts you make will serve you one day: I guarantee it!

Chapter 5
Present Your Corporate Identity

What exactly is your *corporate identity or brand*? What does it consist of? Well these are marketing terms that include many things, all having to do with company imaging and perception. Your corporate identity includes all your marketing collateral—logo, website, brochures, stationery and business cards—how you carry yourself and dress (covered in Part IV), and even what you say when speaking about your business. These things brand your company by providing a certain look and feel that is exclusively you.

YOUR LOGO: A REFLECTION OF YOU
Your logo is the first step in branding your company. We are all familiar with some logos that are famous worldwide, such as those for Microsoft, Nike, McDonald's or Starbucks. Your company may be much smaller that these, but you still need to do what they did—create an image that represents you and makes you stand out in the minds of people with whom you want to do business.

If art class wasn't your most stellar moment in school, find a graphic artist or marketing business to create one for you. The important thing to remember is that this design will appear on almost everything associated with your business. Make it memorable!

BUSINESS CARDS: NEVER LEAVE HOME WITHOUT THEM!

What do you think is the most important piece of marketing collateral your business owns? If you said website, I'd say sorry! How about brochures? Nope.

The most important piece of collateral your business owns is its business card. Does that surprise you? Well the business card is the most used and seen collateral your company owns. People see your business cards more often than websites, brochures or other marketing material.

For this reason, you must invest in creating a business card that stands out and gets noticed. It needs to be unique. If you are just starting a business and have only a limited budget, I recommend creating a nice logo and business card first. Your card will promote you and your business better than anything else.

Websites are important. They create credibility. But I know some very successful consultants that own no marketing material whatsoever, other than a great business card. So you can wait on that website if you have to, but do not attend a networking function without business cards, even if (initially) it's just inexpensive cards made on your personal printer (I'm shuddering as I write this)!

A better alternative if budget is an issue is to select graphic designers that are just starting their own business. They are talented and can design a nice logo and card for you at a great price. How can you find these people? Well, once you've read this book and know how to network, you'll just ask your network. Until then, search your local Chamber of Commerce's online Member Directory for a listing of graphic designers.

Another affordable option is using Vista Print, an online resource that prints all kinds of marketing materials. You can use their business card template. You can also upload logos, if you already have one, and design your card. Shipment is fast. For more information on Vista Print, please go to www.vistaprint.com. I've used them to print my collateral jackets and have always been satisfied with the results. They are also extremely customer service oriented and willing to help.

I hope I've made my point as to the importance of your business card. Mine is designed at an angle and has bold colors. I have rarely handed it out without getting a comment or compliment. It helps people remember me in less than those seven meetings it usually takes to be remembered.

Once you've had your cards printed, always take enough with you when attending a networking event. I'm especially amazed at the seasoned networkers that attend having forgotten their cards. It's very unprofessional. Don't let that happen to you. Actually, you should always carry your business cards wherever you go; you never know where or when you'll meet your next prospect. You should even keep some in your car.

Why are business cards so important?

- They provide your contact information.
- They create credibility for you and your business.
- If they're expensive looking and well designed, they demonstrate success (people want to do business with successful people).
- They show your professionalism.
- They help you get business.
- They help you to be remembered.
- Without them they discount you.

CREATE AND MEMORIZE YOUR COMPANY POSITION STATEMENT

Before you can attend your first networking function, you must be able to tell people what you do in a way that generates interest in no more than 10 to 15 seconds. Here is one easy method for creating your Company Position Statement.

Answer these questions:

1. What do you do?
2. For whom (your target market)?
3. What value does it bring to your clients?
4. What value does it bring your clients' *customers*? This is *most* important to the prospect.

Keep it between 10 and 15 seconds.

Create different Company Position Statements for different audiences as needed.

Example of one of Savar & Associates' Company Position Statements:

We train (#1 above) culturally diverse companies (#2) on how to provide exceptional customer experiences (#1) that earn client loyalty (#4), expand business opportunity and increase bottom-line profitability (#3).

Chapter 6
Define Your Networking Objectives

Once you're armed with a corporate identity, a set of business cards and a carefully prepared Company Position Statement, you're ready to decide what you want to accomplish. It's time to set your networking objectives.

FIRST: SOME BASIC SALES TERMINOLOGY

This section is for individuals interested in attending networking events for the primary purpose of finding prospects and growing their businesses. Your current business or career status, be it finding prospects, finding employment or climbing the corporate ladder, is the motivating factor for determining how you go about networking and selecting the people you choose to target.

For those of you seeking prospects and new business opportunities, let's review a few basic sales terms that may be unfamiliar if you're new to business, networking and sales before we continue discussing your networking strategy. While these terms generally mean the same thing for everyone, your business status (as defined in Chapter 4) will influence how you use them.

Both marketing and sales organizations are tasked with lead generation and identification of qualified prospects. *A prospect is someone who shares with you a goal, objective, challenge or need that your company can address.* The act of looking for prospects is called prospecting.

Lead generation is the identification of potential prospects through a variety of sources. Leads can be generated by your marketing department, a teammate, a client or someone in your network.

Leads generated by your marketing department are usually the results of mass marketing efforts, such as those that come through websites, trade shows, eZines, postcards and flyers.

Salespeople use direct, one-on-one or transactional methods. Old school salespeople still attempt to use outdated methods, such as cold calling—dropping in on a prospect without an appointment—and telemarketing. Sophisticated sales executives recognize that they can elevate their status, work less and achieve more by attending networking functions.

There are circumstances where telemarketing has value, such as verifying business cards received at trade shows before following up. Other than that, I have little use for such outdated methods in today's techno-savvy world where calls are screened, blocked or sent to voice mail, never to be returned.

What about people we meet who do not qualify as prospects? In the sales world, we refer to them as *suspects*. Can a suspect ever become a prospect? Yes! That is why we want to include and stay connected with *everyone* we meet as we build our network. Even if your suspects never convert to prospects, they may still play important roles for you as teaming-alliance partners, provider-partners, virtual sales team members, referral sources and so much more.

Here's an example of a suspect turned prospect. You attend a networking function and meet a couple of people that just left their employment to start their own business. You own or work for a payroll processing company. At this point, they don't need your services. But you stay connected with them. Two years pass and their business has grown to over 50 employees. They now need a payroll processing company. Because you stayed connected, you should be the first person they contact. And you had better close that sale!

WHAT GETS YOUR FOOT IN THE DOOR?

According to a study conducted by the Kenan-Flagler Business School, University of North Carolina, the most successful method for gaining a meeting with a buyer decision-maker is either through direct contact with the decision-maker or through a referral from someone within his or her organization. The second most effective method is a warm introduction (an introduction made in person, by phone or through an e-mail) through an outside person, such as a trusted consultant, to the prospective buyer. The worst method is cold calling (e.g., unannounced visit and telemarketing). Figure 1 below, the summarized results of the Kenan-Flagler study, demonstrates the likelihood of meeting with a buyer based on various scenarios. It ranks the best and worst methods of gaining access to an executive.[1]

---

1   Alston Gardner, Chief Executive Officer, Target Marketing Systems, Inc.; Stephen J. Bistritz, Ed.D., Director of Development, Target Marketing Systems, Inc.; and Jay E. Klompmaker, Ph.D., Professor of Business Administration, Kenan-Flagler Business School, University of North Carolina. "Selling to Senior Executives, How Salespeople Establish Trust and Credibility with Senior Executives," white paper, 1995.

Note: Target Marketing Systems became renamed OnTarget, and was purchased by Siebel in 1999.

FIGURE 1: GAINING ACCESS TO DECISION MAKERS

	ALWAYS	USUALLY	OCCASIONALLY	NEVER
Recommendation from someone inside the company	16%	68%	16%	0%
Referral from outside the company	8%	36%	44%	12%
A contact at an off-site meeting	0%	44%	32%	24%
Letter from salesperson followed by phone call	4%	20%	40%	36%
A direct telephone call from a salesperson	0%	20%	36%	44%

With today's security systems and no-solicitation warnings posted on most buildings, it's risky to just walk into someone's office uninvited and unannounced. The fact that you're dismissing their posting demonstrates your lack of consideration. (Sorry, old school thinkers, but those cold calling days are inappropriate, risky and possibly dangerous in today's security conscious and fearful society.) If you get into the office, the first impression you make is most likely to be a negative one, assuming you even meet the decision-maker. But that's unlikely, because you will probably be blocked by the receptionist or a locked door requiring card access.

Yes, there are some exceptions. Big name companies can sometimes get away with bad behavior. But for the majority, cold calling is tacky and outdated. It reduces you to vendor status, rather than a dignified equal provider-partner, which is more likely to happen if you meet at a networking event. As for telemarketing, it's no better. With Caller ID, screening and transferring into voice mails, it's a demoralizing time waster for the seller.

There is a better way. It's called networking! Believe me, people are much less likely to refuse your call or ignore your e-mail if they met you at a networking function. There is always that very strong possibility that they will run into you again. How embarrassing would that be for them if they had ignored your calls and e-mails!

QUANTIFY YOUR NETWORKING OBJECTIVES

If your goal is to learn how to be a power networker, but you're not responsible for sales or business acquisition, you may skip this section and go directly to Chapter 7: "Target Your Market Segment." This section is for those who are directly responsible for sales or revenue generation, hiring salespeople, setting sales quotas, or determining how much prospecting activity you or your salespeople should be conducting in order to meet or exceed your targeted annual revenue goals.

Consider this a crash course in strategic selling. You cannot be a strategic networker if you don't start with the end in mind—your individual quota or company's targeted annual revenue goal. That means you need to know just how many prospects you must meet in order to close the number of sales required to attain your revenue goals and business objectives. Start by answering these questions:

- What is my annual revenue goal (or individual sales quota)?
- What is my average cost of sale?
- How many sales do I need to meet quota?
- What is my close ratio (or the combined average close ratio of my partners)?
- How many prospects do I need to meet each week, month or year?
- Where do I go to find my prospects?

Set Your Annual Revenue Goals

If your company has already established its annual revenue goals, or if you have an assigned individual sales quota, good job! You may skip this section. If not, this will help you generate answers to create your networking strategy. The easiest way to do this is to begin with the end in mind. What are you trying to accomplish? You want to achieve or surpass a targeted revenue goal.

If you work for a corporation, you are assigned an annual quota. If you are a small business or startup, you are far more likely to achieve success if you set individual and corporate revenue goals and create a networking strategy for achieving it. Lacking a strategy and a defined sales quota is like driving with no destination in mind. Is it any wonder that you never get there? Enough studies have been conducted on goal setting to know that you are far more likely to succeed in your business and career if you take the time to establish your goals. In this case, it's your revenue or sales goals.

Determine How Many Prospects You Need to Make Quota

Let's say your annual sales quota is $1 million and your average sale is $50,000:

$$\$1,000,000 / \$50,000 = 20 \text{ sales transactions}$$

So you need to close 20 sales that average $50,000 each in order to achieve your quota. How many prospects do you need to meet in order to close twenty sales? That number depends on your *close ratio*—the number of proposals you submit to your prospects divided by the number of resulting sales you make or close. Let's say for every four prospects you meet, you submit two proposals and you close one sale:

$$2 \text{ proposals} / 1 \text{ closed sales} = 50\% \text{ close ratio}$$

But how many prospects did you need to close one sale? Based on the above example, you needed to meet four prospects to submit two proposals and close one sale. So how many qualified prospects do you need to meet in order to make your annual quota?

20 sales x 4 prospects per sale = 80 qualified prospects
(40 submitted proposals)

So to achieve your goals, you need to meet eighty good prospects per year, approximately seven per month, or two per week. That should help you plan the number of networking events you need to attend. It is worth repeating here that *a prospect is a person who has shared a challenge, goal, objective or problem with you that your products or services can resolve*. If you know this person's company uses your services but does not share the above information with you, he is not a qualified prospect. Counting him as such will only cause you to fall short in meeting your revenue targets; he won't buy from you until he shares this information with you.

Without a carefully designed strategy, you can attend numerous networking events and not meet a single prospect. Can you now see how so many hard working startups go out of business? Working hard is not enough; you must work smart. You must be strategic. That means that you have to improve the odds of meeting eligible prospects (kind of like dating) by going where your prospects go.

Chapter 7
Target Your Market Segment

As stated earlier, there are literally hundreds of networking functions happening each week, and you can easily go out of business attending functions where your prospects are nowhere to be found. How can you choose the right events and venues to attend? Strategize!

FOCUS ON C-LEVEL EXECUTIVES

Does the price of the networking function matter? Yes it does! You want to meet decision makers, people who can approve a sale or offer you a job. The lower the cost of the function, the more likely you'll meet salespeople rather than senior executives with decision making authority. Even if they don't meet with you, a senior executive's referral to a junior staff member puts you at the top of that employee's to-do list.

That doesn't mean you should never attend less expensive functions, especially if you are an independent or small business owner. These can be good opportunities to meet salespeople (they usually attend these functions) and begin building your virtual sales team. But even then, be sure that the event you select draws salespeople who sell in *your* target industry or market. You can call and inquire about the types of members and guests that usually attend a particular function, or try one out. If you don't meet people of interest, drop this venue from your list.

Do you know why senior executives avoid low cost events like the plague? First, they prefer to network with their peers. But more importantly, it's because following such an event, they are bombarded by entrepreneurs and salespeople requesting meetings. The worst part, I am told, is that more often than not, the people making these requests have failed to do any prior research to first determine whether the executive's company is a viable prospect. Shame on anyone who does that! It's totally unprofessional and reflects poorly on the individual and the company they represent.

C-Level on a Budget

If you have a limited networking budget, choose events where C-level executives go (CEO, CIO, CFO, COO). If for example, you have a monthly networking budget of $300, attend a couple of lower-priced events so that you can expand your network by meeting vendors, provider-partners, virtual sales team partners, referrals, etc. Also attend at least two higher priced events that you have carefully targeted as venues where you are most likely to meet C-level decision makers—and not your competitors.

It's better to select and attend two of the more expensive functions (over $100) than to attend ten low priced events. You should know why by now—decision makers attend the more expensive events. Go where your decision makers go!

Relationships at C-Level

As you make contacts with the decision-makers, also begin to build relationships with them. Don't act desperate for their business, and don't be pushy. People want to do business with successful people, so show confidence and look for ways to offer value by helping them first. Research and understand their businesses so you can converse intelligently about both their company and their individual business goals and objectives.

Remember, unsophisticated salespeople *present* (monologue) to decision makers and focus on the features and benefits of their products and services. They usually get delegated to the level of their conversation, generally a middle level manager with budget constraints and limited buying authority.

If you want to build relationships with top level executives, you must learn to speak their language. Partner with them and build relationships by *conversing—rather than presenting*—to uncover their needs, challenges, goals and objectives. Only then can you align your products or services to recommend and propose the best solutions that meet their needs.

Help C-levels achieve their business objectives, and you'll earn a reputation as someone who is not only business savvy, but also authentic, helpful and sincere. You'll be regarded as a person of integrity.

Once you have won them over, you will get their business. Let your competitors go through the tedious, costly and time-consuming traditional sales process of responding to Requests For Proposal (RFPs). That's how sales decisions are made at the lower and middle levels, not at the top.

IDENTIFY THE RIGHT VENUES AND ORGANIZATIONS

Let's examine industries, associations, clubs, chambers of commerce and other organizations that host networking functions.

Your Industry's Associations

It's a good idea to join your industry's professional association. It provides training in your field of business, connects you to other people in your industry, creates contacts for future job opportunities and can often lead to referrals. For example, let's say you join the American Marketing Association and develop a strong relationship with someone from a large marketing firm. Such firms usually have large companies for clients. You're a startup, happy to get any business that comes your way. Having developed a relationship with you the larger will be more inclined to refer smaller prospects to you. Remember, people do business with and give business to people they like.

By networking within your industry's association you can make valuable contacts that can provide a wealth of resources for you. Some of the best jobs and career opportunities will come to you through your industry's association. By joining and getting actively involved, you'll never have to worry about unemployment again: you've got a network to help you land that next great job.

Referral Sharing Organizations and Associations

These organizations' exclusive purpose is to bring businesspeople together for lead exchange. Most of these organizations only allow one person per industry to attend the group. This is important; you don't want your competitors there as well. These groups meet weekly with the purpose of sharing information about their business and their needs, spotlight a company each week and submit any leads they have come across to the appropriate group members. By the way, most active Chambers of Commerce offer referral sharing groups as part of membership.

Groups such as these are good for entrepreneurs, and small companies. They can be a good way to get referrals from group members and build your virtual sales team. The disadvantage is that sometimes many of the attending members are in such diverse businesses that they do not call on your targeted customer base. Also, participants are not always buyers and decision-makers, so it is hit or miss. I know people who claim to receive great leads that result in sales from these referral sharing organizations. Others have not been so lucky.

Some referral sharing organizations are quite expensive for entrepreneurs and start-up businesses, so I recommend that you go and try them out before joining. You can go on your own or be invited by an existing member. Depending on the organization, most will let you attend a few times before requiring you to become a member. Many referral sharing groups hold multiple meetings on different days, times and locations, so if you attend one and don't find it valuable, try another at a different location before making your final decision.

For a listing of some of the more well known referral sharing organizations, please refer to the Resource list in the Appendix.

Organizations That Have Your Prospects as Members

The most financially rewarding networking venues are organizations and associations attended by *your prospects*. There you are not among competitors, but potential buyers. You want to go where your prospects go, not where your competitors are more likely to be found. What markets have you targeted? For example, if you've targeted the legal sector to sell software specific to that industry, go to events where your prospective clients are most likely to be found, such as the American Bar Association's local chapter events or, if you can afford it, their national conferences.

If you want to sell to the financial sector and are not certain where to find your prospects, do an Internet search on "Financial Associations," "Financial Organizations" or "Financial Institutions." Select the organization that best meets your objectives and attend an event sponsored by their local chapter (their website should list their calendar of upcoming events). Try attending one of the more expensive events—$50 to $150 for a breakfast, lunch or dinner— because that's where you're more likely to meet decision makers. Evaluate the venue to determine whether this is a group you wish to get involved with further. We'll discuss "involvement" shortly.

Business Clubs

If you can afford to join a business club, do it. There are so many advantages. First, it's among the easiest venues for meeting C-level executive decision makers, as they are usually club members.

Because you are also a member, you have elevated status and are addressed on a personal—and formal—basis and treated royally by the staff, just like the people you want to meet. You appear successful, and people want to do business with successful people. It increases your value and assures them you will not be out of business tomorrow. That reduces risk for the cautious low-risk buyers and gives you a competitive advantage over other small, non-member companies.

Invite your prospects to lunch at your business club. It gives you the home court advantage. Going to a client's office puts you at an immediate disadvantage; there is inequity between the relationships, and they control how you are treated. That's fine if they are courteous. But if they're not, they think nothing of keeping you waiting, interrupting your meeting by taking a call or even responding to an e-mail. What's the message here? To me it says you are a devalued vendor, not a valued provider-partner. I choose not to do business with people who attempt to treat me in such a manner. Such situations are never perceived (by the prospective client) as a partnership and therefore a relationship is very unlikely to develop. Without that, there is no building of trust or integrity. This almost always results in a win-lose, which is ultimately a lose-lose for both. Always try to conduct business with prospects at your club to alleviate this scenario.

When you invite your prospect to your business club, you're in control. In your exclusive business setting, most prospects judge you differently—more as a partner and peer—treat you with respect and are less likely to attempt to haggle or negotiate your fair price. And they'll feel confident giving you their business, because they feel you're worth it! Business clubs also offer:

- Facilities (phones, PC with Internet connections, faxes, printers, etc.) to hold meetings and conduct your business on site. This is a great set-up for the self-employed that sometimes need an office away from home.

- Fine dining (What better way to build relationships than over a casual, deliciously prepared meal?).

- Monthly billing, so there is no discomfort over paying the check.

- Added bonus: If you are married, some business clubs give you two for the price of one. Bring your spouse to meet and dine with other couples. You build friendships and business partnerships. Several very senior corporate executives have shared with me that most of their company's business and closest friendships came through the couples they befriended with their spouses over the years at our business club.

Country Clubs

You can make some great networking contacts by meeting your neighbors and community club members. Most club members are employed, are successful and can be great contacts to add to your network. You are as likely to get business and leads by the people you meet at your country club as you are at your business club—maybe more so; since people in your community come together to socialize and are focusing on building friendships rather than business relationships. As friendships develop and you learn about each others' business, you're far more likely to help your friend get business than a simple business acquaintance.

Toastmasters International

Are you familiar with this worldwide organization? If you have career aspirations of any kind, you are going to need good communication skills and are going to have to speak publicly at some point, be it in the form of public relations, a networking function, a sales presentation, or business or board meetings.

Public speaking is ranked as people's number one fear! Toastmasters International has thousands of chapters worldwide, and its mission is to help people get over their fear of public speaking and become more confident and relaxed speakers. The environment is friendly and supportive. After your presentation group members give feedback in a positive, non-judgmental, non-critical manner. To find a meeting near you and learn more about this excellent organization, please see their information in the Appendix.

Meetings are specified as being either "open to the public" or "closed for employees." So let's discuss how Toastmasters can also be a great networking venue for you. Earlier I said to go where your prospects go. Many Toastmasters meetings are held in government facilities and large corporations. Check to see if any of your prospective companies hold open Toastmasters meetings. If so, attend at those locations. You'll conquer your fear of public speaking while making great contacts with employees of the company or government agency you wish to penetrate. That's called getting in through the back door.

THE VALUE IN ACTIVE COMMUNITY SERVICE

Getting involved is great for your community and your business. Select an organization that is near and dear to you and *get involved* by joining one or more of their committees. For me it's the United Way and the Orphan Foundation of America. There are so many advantages to selecting and getting actively involved with the charity organization of your choice. Here are a few:

- Potential buyers like to do business with community service minded companies.

- It's the best place to meet senior executives when you are not one! Most senior corporate executives are required to participate in community service, because they understand it's good for their business. When you join a committee, you develop relationships with people you otherwise would never have had the opportunity to meet. They become a part of your network. You can call on each other to help with a host of needs, including prospects and referrals. Where else can you get an opportunity to sit next to a senior vice president or CEO of a major company when you're just a little startup?

- Community service is a great way to grow your business by making contacts with key decision-makers. And all the while you're feeling great because you're giving back to your community.

THE PAYOFF OF COMMITTEE VOLUNTEERISM

Here's that key point again: The average person needs seven introductions before he or she is remembered. Just joining an organization or non-profit is insufficient for reducing those odds. To more quickly gain notice and visibility by the entire membership, you need to *get involved*. How? Join a committee.

Every business association, organization or non-profit depends primarily on volunteerism. Each has committees that need volunteers. If you're a marketing professional, join the marketing and communications committee. If you're in sales, join the new membership committee. You not only get to meet and develop relationships with other committee members who become a part of your network, but you have access to the membership as well. For those tasked with revenue generation and business expansion, that's a great list to have! Of course you must use it discreetly and within the code of ethics specified by the organization. I've met great prospects and closed good business by joining committees, and it definitely helped me to become known throughout the organization very quickly.

Joining an organization without getting involved in a committee is an inefficient use of your time and membership fees. But join only as many as you can remain actively involved with while doing your day job. People have a tendency to keep asking more from those that do the most. So set your limits. You do not earn respect by agreeing to all requests. Don't allow anyone to talk you into committing to something you do not want to do.

The length of time and the commitment levels vary depending on the position. I serve on the United Way's Regional Advisory Council. We meet monthly, but there is no mandatory term (though a year's commitment is appreciated). It's worth noting that the higher the level of your volunteerism within an organization, the more visibility you have among the organization's members and the more likely that your committee volunteers are more senior level executives (i.e. decision makers). In any case, understand the responsibilities and time commitments before you sign on.

HOW TO DETERMINE WHETHER TO STAY OR WALK AWAY FROM A COMMITTEE OR AN ORGANIZATION

Time is money. How long should your commitment be in order to see some return on your time investment? If you are investing a great deal of time and not getting any business from it, you have a decision to make, especially if you are a small business owner who wears all the company hats. It's easy to go out of business while trying to serve others.

It has to be a win-win. I recommend that you give it six months, unless a position requires a one year commitment. In that case I suggest you never accept that type of commitment until you first work with the organization to ensure a good fit. If after six months you have not received any leads, referrals, or something of business value (such as a teaming alliance, job opportunity or career change), you cannot afford to continue unless you are truly dedicated to serving the specific cause without seeking the business payoff. That is, of course, a personal decision.

Most businesses die in the first five years because they spend too much time doing work that does not generate revenue. If you're not selling, you cannot sustain your business. Networking through organizations, non-profits and events helps put you in front of prospects and decision makers. It is your best chance for growth. Your ultimate, number one focus, must be your business. If you are involved in an organization that is not creating a win-win, move on.

Please see the Resources section in the Appendix for a listing of some of the many nationally recognized organizations.

Part III Highlights

- Your networking strategy consists of:
  - Setting annual revenue goals (quotas) and objectives
  - Targeting your market segment
  - Creating and memorizing your Company Position Statement
- To determine the number of networking events you must attend, you must first calculate the number of sales you need in order to meet your annual quota or targeted business revenue goals.
- Identify which organizations are best suited for finding your prospects and gaining maximum benefit from membership.
- To become known more quickly within the organizations you join (always a networking goal) become active in a committee that utilizes your talents and strengths.
- Save time and money by strategically selecting the right venues for meeting the buyer decision-maker. Select the more expensive networking events; that's where you're most likely to meet the buyers and decision makers you seek.
- Less expensive networking events draw lower level business-people. These are not to be discounted; you can use these contacts to build your virtual sales team, find business provider-partners and vendors.

- If you have a limited budget, attend at least one more expensive (over $75) networking event each month. You won't meet the CEO's of major corporations, but you will meet CEO's of small and middle-sized companies. They will need your services as well.

- Review the amount of business you received from organizations you've joined to determine whether to continue or place your efforts where they will be better served. Depending on your average sales cycle, evaluate after three to six months.

- Always focus on meeting the decision-maker. Top executives are members of business and social clubs. Become a member if you can afford it.

- Get involved in charitable non-profit organizations and community service programs, and be sure to volunteer on a committee. Not only is it important to give back to your community, it will create opportunities for meeting high-level decision makers and corporate executives.

PART IV

The Networking Process

Chapter 8
The Art of Networking

You've created your winning networking strategy—the science of networking—using a logical, well-defined action plan. Now let's discuss your networking process, which is part science and part art. The science behind the process is its series of steps that, when performed often and evaluated repeatedly, results in your performance excellence. The art is in the mastery of soft skills, such as appearance and first impressions, confidence, communication and etiquette. As you master networking, your professionalism, efficiency, productivity, and name recognition will increase exponentially.

Creating a networking process begins by creating your distinctive professional brand that sets you apart from others. Your professional brand consists of how you dress, sound, act and even how you enter the room. You must know how to create the right mix of approachability (body language, smile) and credibility (business attire, confidence) for the networking event you're attending.

You must know which individuals and groups to approach, which to avoid and how to engage and disengage gracefully with people you meet. Most importantly, your networking success requires an understanding of business etiquette and impeccable manners, so you are noticed for being extraordinary.

Becoming a power networker requires continuous self-evaluation. You cannot improve without it. You must evaluate your performance after each networking event until it becomes second nature to you. Then you'll know you have achieved that status of being a power networker.

EIGHT STEPS TO SUCCESSFUL NETWORKING

Now let's have some fun! Have you ever heard the expression, "We're not here to have fun, but there's no reason why we can't have fun while we're here!" Networking events are the perfect places for this positive attitude.

Let's imagine you are going to an evening networking function that you have strategically selected. There are eight steps you must take to ensure a successful outcome:

Before the Event

1. Dress for success.
2. Decide whether to take a colleague or go solo.
3. Prepare mentally and set goals.

At the Event

4. Enter the networking venue.
5. Don't ogle the feast.
6. Plan your approach.
7. Greet your prospects.
8. Conduct an engaging dialogue and disengage gracefully.

Let's focus first on what to do before you arrive at the event.

Chapter 9
Before the Networking Event

The best way to ensure success at a networking event is to take the time to prepare for it. Think about the nature of the event you're attending and plan for it using this strategy as a guideline to complete the following three steps.

STEP 1: DRESS FOR SUCCESS

What you wear must project the image and message you want to send. Do you want your style to demonstrate credibility, approachability or something in between? That largely depends on the type of networking function you are attending.

A very casual style, including attire, may indicate approachability, but it will not generate the confidence necessary for someone to want to do business with you. At the other extreme, a very conservative style and attire may promote confidence and authority, but could intimidate others from wanting to approach or work with you. Before I continue my discussion on the importance of impeccable grooming, let's take a look at first impressions.

How First Impressions are Formed

Surprisingly, the words we speak are the least important factor in making first impressions:

Visual 55%
Appearance & body language

Non-Verbal 38%
Vocal, sub-vocals, tonality

Verbal 7%
The actual words

Notice that 55 percent of first impressions are made based on the visual. This includes clothing (style and quality), hair, make-up, body language, attitude, etc. Next is the non-verbal, which includes tone (pitch) and sub-vocals ("uh-huh"). Exceptional communicators know when and how to use both for maximum effectiveness. For example, if you wish to convey warmth, you raise your pitch. Smiling causes that to happen automatically. But if you're trying to make a serious point, you drop your pitch—and drop the smile—to convey your authority and credibility.

By far the least important criteria when forming impressions is verbal communications. We've all heard the expression, "It's not what you say but how (tone, body language) you say it."[2]

Does Appearance Really Matter?

Yes! People notice both the style and quality of what you wear. We live in a visual world, and first visual impressions are lasting impressions.

---

2   Nicholas Boothman, *How to Make People Like You in 90 Seconds or Less*, Workman Publishing Company, New York, 2002, page 80.

Note: These statistics have been quoted in numerous publications as well as television shows and are accepted by leading authorities.

People subconsciously use appearance to make inferences and draw conclusions. Once an opinion is formed, it's hard to undo.

Many networking functions list the dress code as business casual. Always dress a notch or two above everyone else. Your goal is to get noticed quickly, not in the seven times it takes the *average* person to be noticed. So leave others to wear business casual. You wear a quality suit. I've noticed some women attempt to differentiate themselves by always wearing something that serves as their unique brand or identifier, such as a broach, hat, or scarf. That's a great idea as long as it doesn't have the opposite, unintended effect—discounted credibility.

I've also known a few men who use their business attire and grooming to differentiate themselves and make lasting impressions. Since most men do not expend as much time and effort in their appearance as women do, those few that do really stand out and get noticed quickly by investing in the quality and attractiveness of their business attire and grooming. So men, if you want to increase the odds of getting noticed quickly, dress impeccably.

Following many of my presentations on networking, I'm often approached by men and women with questions about networking specifics. Several younger people tell me they have a hard time being taken seriously because of their age. What if you are young and just starting out or you just look much younger and are finding it difficult getting prospects to take you seriously?

I had a client who faced this challenge. She was in her early thirties but looked closer to twenty. Although she had ten years of technology experience, she was not being taken seriously by most prospective buyers, both men and women. She shared this problem with me at one of my seminars. Here is what I advised her to do (Note that some of these suggestions apply to both genders.):

- Wear a dark suit to increase credibility and authority.

- Get a great hair cut or wear it up if it's past shoulder length. This young woman had long, very straight hair that made her look even younger.

- Wear make-up. This is a *must* for every professional woman. Not wearing make-up looks like you forgot to finish dressing. Its equivalent to a man dressed in a suit and tennis shoes. No matter how beautiful your suit is, without make-up, you appear poorly groomed and unprofessional.

- Wear a pair of non-prescription glasses to look older (applies to both genders).

At our next seminar she reported that she had taken my advice. The results led to scheduling several meetings with prospects!

A young man once approached me at a networking function. He too had difficulty being taken seriously by older decision makers. He looked younger than his 32 years and wore a slightly spiked, gel-filled hair style. This may look "cool" but it definitely does not create a professional business appearance—even worse since his prospects were primarily government and military personnel! I suggested that he remove the gel and wear his hair in a more natural style. This small change landed big results. Like it or not, people do judge a book by its cover. So create your own unique, professional brand.

Following are separate lists of tips for women and men to create their professional brands and make favorable, lasting impressions. Of course, if you are in the fashion or other artistic industry, you can get away with wearing far more stylish, less conservative clothes than I describe below—attire for traditional business networking functions. But regardless of the business setting, I want you to be noticed by looking your best!

Tips for Women

- Wear a suit. Dark suits and bold colors convey credibility, authority and confidence. Pastel colors, especially pink are discounting. Pink is associated with youth. Little girls wear it because it is cute. Pink is never associated with any adjectives that command authority, credibility, confidence or respect. If you love pink, wear the bold version—fuchsia.

- Nylons are *a must* when wearing a suit or dress. Bare legs discount your professional appearance. So no excuses, even if its 110 degrees outside, you are networking inside.

- Make sure your clothes are not suggestive or seductive. You want decision makers to focus on your *ability and credibility*. If they are looking at any part of your body other than your face, then they are *not hearing your message*.

- Wear clothes that complement, not detract from, your appearance. Avoid flashy clothes, short skirts, spandex, stained clothing, jeans and T-shirts. You don't want to look like one of Madonna's back-up singers. Women who dress too revealingly either don't know better because they are young, or they lack confidence in their ability to deal with men as equals. They only know how to get attention by using their sexuality. This will backfire.

  I remember being at a business club and meeting a woman who was a small business owner. She wore a white shirt that was unbuttoned so low, half of her black bra (and breasts) were clearly revealed. I found it very disconcerting. As a businesswoman, I also found it demeaning. Mostly I was embarrassed for her. That's a sad way to do business. She deserved better and so do we.

- A great haircut is an essential part of looking well groomed. It can be your crowning glory and a differentiator. This does not mean wearing hairstyles best left to fashion models. You want to stand out, but in a positive way.

- Wear appropriate business shoes. Flat shoes, slippers, spiked heels (worse if they're open-heeled) or sandals are not appropriate business footwear. Business shoes can be open toed, but they need a closed or at least strapped heel. Shoes should have at least a two-inch heel, but excessive height is inappropriate. If you're in doubt, ask the shoe salesperson to help you. It's very important that your shoes complement your suit. And always make sure they are polished. People do notice.

- Limit jewelry and accessories. Again you want the focus on your face and message. Anything that distracts from that hurts your business and your professional brand. People should be focusing on you, not distracted by your accessories. Don't wear large, garish jewelry. Dangling earrings are not business attire, but if you are wearing delicate, dangling earrings (no longer than an inch) don't wear a necklace with it. It's overkill. When it comes to jewelry, less is more. You'll look more professional and tastefully dressed.

- Use smaller purses. They create an elegant and well-groomed image.

- To look exceptional, get regular manicures. A French manicure is elegant and professional. It looks good everywhere. Bright (red, orange, fuchsia) or dark (brown, black) colored nails are discounting. Save those fun colors for your social affairs. Think I'm being too picky? Believe me, people notice.

- Create your own unique brand. I know a consultant that always wears a beautiful scarf with her well tailored suits. It's her calling card—her unique brand—and it makes her memorable.

Tips for Men

Now let me address men's clothing. Because many men don't seem to pay much attention to their appearance, you have a real competitive advantage to stand out and be noticed. All it takes is a little more effort to go from ordinary to extraordinary and become unforgettable! I know only a handful of men who fall into this category as I shared with you earlier. They definitely stand out at every function.

Men, to create your *professional brand* and make favorable and lasting impressions:

- Burn your Dockers! At least never wear them to networking events or anywhere else at work.

- If money is a factor, you can buy great looking suits at outlet malls or during sales. Make certain your suits are always laundered and not wrinkled or stained. Buy quality over quantity. People can tell the difference, especially senior executives.

- Invest in long-sleeved shirts, even in summer. Leave short-sleeved shirts for little boys to wear. *Don't buy button-down (at the collar) shirts.* That has middle-management written all over it. It's better to have a few more expensive shirts than many of lower quality. Beautiful shirts get noticed.

- Buy ties in bold and bright colors, suggesting your own boldness, confidence and leadership. Again focus on quality.

- Buy nice looking business shoes, and keep them polished. If you're uncertain about selecting the right pair of shoes, ask a salesperson for help.

- A great haircut is a must, and don't forget to accompany it with your engaging smile!

- If you have the confidence, get your nails manicured.

- If you do all of the above, people will think you are a senior executive.

Tips for Everyone

- *Dress for the impression you want to make!*

- *Dress for the people you want to meet!*

- *Dress for the job you want to have!*

Tip from an image consultant: Update your eyewear, wear a first class watch, shine your shoes, whiten your teeth and wear a beautiful smile!

Before we move on to Step 2, I want to share with you that we learn from our mistakes, not our successes. Many of the tips I shared above, especially for my female readers are the result of my own mistakes and learning experiences. I hope to save you time, money—and embarrassment—by keeping you looking your best.

STEP 2: PREPARE FOR THE NETWORKING EVENT

Mental Preparation is as Important as Physical Preparation

Its 6:00 p.m. as you pull into the parking lot of the networking function. You've been up since 6:00 a.m. and have had a hectic day at work. Are you looking forward to this networking event? Most people, if they're being honest, would answer with a resounding no!

Most of us would rather be anywhere else, like at home with the family, the family dog, the neighbor's dog, reading a book or just watching TV while sipping a nice cold glass of Pinot Grigio or beer. But that won't help us get good business, will it?

A tired, negative or grumpy attitude will not only not help, it will hinder your networking success. To be an effective networker, you have to be consistent with your *professional brand*. We already discussed creating your professional brand as it pertains to image and appearance. Now let's focus on its equally important counterparts—attitude and confidence! One surefire way of differentiating yourself is to come across as a warm, friendly, helpful and confident person.

So now let's get you into the networking mood. But how are you supposed to do that when you've had such a rotten day or are just plain exhausted? Here are some tricks to use to get you in the networking mood.

Create Your Positive Attitude!

Your attitude is a choice you make. It is controlled by the quality of your thoughts. Negative thoughts create negative feelings and emotions (experienced physically such as a knot in your stomach) and result in negative attitudes. People with negative attitudes project negative body language and attract negative experiences. The same holds true for positive attitudes. Just as negative thoughts lead to negative attitudes, positive thoughts lead to positive ones. People with positive attitudes project positive body language and attract positive experiences. So how can you change your thoughts to create a more positive attitude that helps put you in a networking mood?

This is a trick I use to get myself in the networking mood. Once you have arrived at the function, and while you are still in your parked car, begin to create your positive attitude by looking in the rearview mirror and smiling, even if you don't feel like it. Do this a few times until you burst out laughing (I promise you will), and you will actually feel your bad mood dissolving.

If you think I've lost it, let me share this online article in "Time in Partnership with CNN." Here's an excerpt:

> *It might actually make you happier to smile. Based on the psychology that a person feels whatever emotion they are acting at the moment, you will probably feel better if you smile. To avoid what is called cognitive dissonance, in which our thoughts and actions don't match up, our minds react to the change in our facial expression to bring our beliefs in line with our behavior. And, like laughter, it's contagious. If you smile, chances are that those around you will too.[3]*

You cannot maintain a bad mood when you're laughing!

Set Your Networking Goals

Here's the second trick I use when I'm not in the networking mood: I set a networking goal. If the function is from 6:00 to 9:00 p.m., and you feel blah about being there, choose one of the following options:

a. Set the length of time you will stay—at least one hour—and promise yourself that you will be an effective networker during that time. That way when you're ready to leave, you'll know you've done your best.

---

3   Time in Partnership with CNN, "Smile," Time in Partnership with CNN, Health and Happiness. <http://www.time.com/time/specials/2007/article/0,28804,1631176_1630611_1630630,00. html>, (August 2007).

b. Set a goal based on the number of contacts you'll make before you leave. You determine the type of contacts. They can be all prospects or a combination of prospects, alliances, and referral partners. Once you've achieved that number, you can leave.

By using either of the above methods, you will feel good about yourself, know you did your best and feel responsible about doing what needs to be done to promote your business.

By the way, don't forget to take enough business cards with you! I'm amazed when I attend functions and meet people who have actually forgotten to bring their business cards with them. It really creates an unprofessional impression.

Turn Off Your Cell Phone!

Technology has changed our lives in amazing ways. We have come to rely on our cell phones to stay in constant contact with our network of friends and business associates. Cell phones are life savers in cases of emergency. But technological strengths also have their flip side. The cell phone becomes a weakness—defined as a strength carried to the extreme—when used inappropriately, such as while driving in heavy traffic or when using it while attending a networking event.

There is nothing that states "non-executive pretending to be important" than someone who walks into a room with a cell phone or PDA attached to their ear. Cell phones and networking events just don't mix. They discount you and your professionalism. It's best to leave them in the car. If you have an emergency and must carry it, put it on vibrate before leaving your car. Do not even use your cell phone in the parking lot; you are being noticed by others. When you see a person approaching and speaking on a cell phone, what impression does that make? Do you see this person as a senior executive? I do not. I see him or her as an overworked salesperson or a small to middle sized business owner, maybe believing that the number of calls they receive demonstrates their importance and business success.

Regardless of your position, you want to project an image that commands respect and authority. You want to be able to partner with any level executive, so you must project the part of a senior executive. You never know who is watching you and forming a negative impression.

Unfortunately, there have been no etiquette books written on how to conduct ourselves in today's rapidly changing technology. But when you are talking to a person and you answer your cell phone, you are letting that person know that he or she is less important than the caller. If that is the case, then why are you there with this person and not with the caller? The person you are physically with *always* takes priority over a phone call. Isn't that why cell phones offer the convenience of voice mail?

While cell phones play valuable roles in our lives, there is a time and a place for everything. Make your cell phone a friend, not a foe.

STEP 3: DECIDE WHETHER TO BRING A FRIEND OR GO SOLO

It helps to bring a friend or friends when you're nervous about attending networking functions, as long as you do not stick together. That defeats the whole purpose. It will be harder for you to move around the room and talk to people or for people to feel comfortable enough to approach. You don't want to end up by the food table eating, drinking and socializing with your friend or your fellow employees. If you do, here are some messages you may inadvertently be sending to others:

1. This is a private conversation. Do not approach.

2. We don't want to be here, so we are going to eat and drink and make the most of it.

3. We won't go out of our way to approach people, but should you venture over, feel free to join us.

4. If you do join us, you may be overwhelmed by the experience of being outnumbered and by our attempts to sell to you.

5. We are so friendly that you will feel like the sacrificial lamb.

So if you are planning to go to a function with one or more business associates, make your time count and circulate individually to gain the greatest benefit from the event. Go to opposite sides of the room and work inward toward one another. That way you can meet most of the people in the room.

Chapter 10

During the Networking Event:
Meeting and Greeting

You've dressed well, created a positive attitude and decided whether to bring someone along. Now you have arrived. It's show time!

STEP 4: ENTER THE NETWORKING VENUE

As you arrive, project an air of confidence. It's a must and gets you noticed instantly. Displaying a confident attitude says you know your value and your worth. People believe about us what we believe about ourselves. If you appear shy and insecure, others will judge you as lacking credibility. Confidence gains you instant credibility.

How do you display confidence? Start with your positive attitude and smile. Posture is very important so stand tall with your shoulders back but relaxed (down—not up high), and walk with a purposeful stride.

But, what if you're not confident? Do exactly what I said above and "fake it 'til you make it!" Pretend you are a great actor playing the role of a confident person. Believe me, if you do something long enough, it will become second nature to you. So if you initially have to fake confidence by acting, don't worry. The positive responses you'll get from people will actually encourage you and make you more confident.

Now that you're ready, walk over to the registration booth. If you pre-registered, give your name to receive a badge with your name and company name printed on it. Be warm and gracious to the people handling the registration. Acknowledge their hard work and the wonderful job they've done. Whether they are volunteers or paid employees, noticing and showing your appreciation for their hard work creates a favorable and lasting impression. Just that little gesture can make their day. Being nice will be remembered favorably. Remember, these people can also play an important role in your networking circle.

Where to Wear Your Name Tag

Most right and left handed people shake hands with using their right hand. If you are one of these people, place tag just under your right shoulder collar bone. If you shake hands using your left hand, do the same on your left hand side. When you extend your arm to shake hands, it creates a visual line that leads right to your name.

STEP 5: DON'T OGLE THE FEAST (OR BEAST!)

I attend many networking functions, and I notice a lot of people eating and drinking. Those are generally the amateurs and the nervous (okay, and starved), not the power networkers.

Should I Eat?

There are several problems with eating at networking receptions. First, how do you shake hands if you have a glass of wine or soda in one hand and a plate of food in the other? And if this person asks you a question and your mouth is full of delicious appetizers, it's going to be awkward, embarrassing and very unprofessional. People do notice, especially decision makers—the people you are trying to meet—and who most likely are not eating.

You're probably upset with me because after all, its dinner time and you're starving. Plus there's all that scrumptious food there! They expect you to eat. They don't want to waste money, right?

I once had a person at one of my presentations ask me why, then, were they paying for the networking event if they shouldn't eat? What do you think I answered? You are paying for business opportunities! It's called net*work* for a reason: we're there primarily to *work*, not to socialize.

Here is my compromise. Remember the networking goal you set back in your car? Once you've achieved it, let the food be your reward. But even then, don't overdo. You are still being observed, whether you realize it or not, and you always want to make a lasting, positive impression. Plus, someone could still walk up to you, and there you are right back where we started from: drink in one hand, food in the other!

Should I Drink? What About Alcohol?

It takes a really confident person to stand there with no glass and no food in hand. Most people feel less conspicuous holding refreshments. That's fine as long as your other hand is free to shake hands. But are we talking soft drinks or alcohol?

Your objective is to create your unique, professional brand that gets you noticed more quickly. If you are a person who can take a glass of wine and carry it all evening, by all means have a drink. If on the other hand, one glass of alcohol puts you in a party mood and makes you want to keep on drinking, please stick with soft drinks! If you want to feel more elegant, ask for sparkling water in a wine glass.

Alcohol can also turn a good networking opportunity into a pick-up scene for both men and women who overindulge. People who have had a few drinks can say things that are inappropriate in a business environment. Someone who has tried to "pick you up" (or someone you've tried to pick up) is very unlikely to give you any business. So be careful and use good judgment. It takes only moments to damage your reputation but what feels like a lifetime to rebuild it.

STEP 6: PLAN YOUR APPROACH

You have registered, and you're wearing your badge, positive attitude, and smile. You enter the room exuding warmth and confidence. What now?

What Do I Do if I Brought Someone With Me?

What you do depends on whether the person is a fellow employee or a business associate. I would not bring non-professional, personal friends to a networking function. It will discount your value.

You and a fellow employee both work for the same company and are there for the same reasons. You can maximize the return on your networking investment by splitting up once you enter the network reception. Start on opposite ends of the room and work your way inward. That way between you, you can meet a majority of the people without duplicating efforts. You can then compare notes and follow up on leads the next day.

A business associate is a business person who does not work with you in your company but is familiar with your work. If you've used each other's services then all the better. In this scenario, work the room together. As you meet people, *sell each others' business services*. It's so much easier to brag about or compliment someone else's accomplishments. This is extremely effective for small business owners.

For example, I am a motivational trainer and speaker. I attend a networking function with my provider-partner who owns a marketing business. We have used each other's services. Rather than talk about our own product and service offerings, we praise the other's offerings. This adds tremendous credibility. Who are you more likely to trust about my great presentation skills—me or the testimony of someone who attended my presentation?

Who to Approach First, Second or Not at All

Who should you approach first? If you're nervous, the easiest way to get over your fear is to help another person get over his or hers.

Singles First

If you're a novice networker and nervous yourself, or if you just want to put yourself in a great networking mood, approach the singles first. These people are the most shy and nervous, and your acts of kindness will be appreciated and noticed. So resolve to approach those who appear uncomfortable or shy first. Helping them get over their fear will take your mind off your own and build your confidence as well.

How do you find those people in need of your help? Look around the circumference of the room. What do you see? In almost every networking function I've attended, I see terrified people standing against the wall, wishing they were anywhere else. Most likely they are new business owners who have never sold before and have attended few if any prior networking events. They are now responsible for revenue generation, and they have attended alone. These are the people you want to rescue—I mean help—first. Why?

- They are very nervous.

- They don't know what to do.

- They want and would appreciate your help.

- It will take your mind off of your own networking fears.

- Helping others is rewarding and will be remembered and appreciated long after the function ends.

- One of these people might be a diamond in the rough. He or she may know someone you want to meet.

- Its great practice for you and practice leads to perfection!

As you go about the room networking, pay attention to the business needs of the people you meet. Then when you get a match (seller of a service and buyer in need of this service), make the appropriate introductions. They may have networked all evening and never run into each other. Your simple act of caring and consideration pays huge future dividends. My rule is to always give before you get (take). By focusing on helping others succeed first, you will be noticed, remembered and appreciated. Over time, you will be rewarded for your generosity of spirit.

Threesomes Next

The next group to approach is the threesomes. But how do you become a part of their group while they're deep in conversation? You simply ease your way slowly into their circle, smiling at everyone, without interrupting the conversation. Eventually, when their conversation ends, one of the group members will turn to you and ask you what you do. You are then part of the group.

Regardless of your level of networking confidence, never approach and interrupt a group and take over the conversation. Confidence does not replace or excuse bad manners!

Couples

Unless you are a very confident networker, I recommend you initially avoid couples. It's hard to tell whether they know each other personally and are having a private conversation. So until you gain more experience, avoid them unless they approach or invite you to join them.

Larger Groups

Groups of five or more are also groups to avoid. Usually one person is dominating the conversation, and everyone else is a captive audience. You won't get much out of it, so keep your distance. However, you can try standing on the periphery and listening in. If you hear several people speaking, join in as demonstrated in the threesome above. Also, if you spot someone in the group trying to diplomatically work his or her way out, you can give him or her a reason to escape—I mean disengage!

STEP 7: OFFER A CONFIDENT GREETING

You are now ready to begin the actual art of networking. Let's say you spot a woman standing by herself against the wall. You can see she is nervous and shy by her body language and lack of eye contact. Let's start with her and approach her with compassion and warmth.

Smile and Demonstrate Congruency

Smile as you approach to help put both of you at ease. Demonstrate congruency by ensuring that your visual (including body language), verbal and vocal (includes sub-vocal and pitch) cues are all congruent, sending the same positive message. You don't want to be out of sync. For example, if you approach without smiling (negative visual), shake hands (positive visual) and say, "It's nice to meet you" (positive verbal) in a flat tone of voice (negative vocal) with folded arms (negative visual), you're sending incongruent signals, which are confusing at best. The example alone confused me!

When people are in doubt, they judge us by the visual and vocal rather than the verbal cues. Mixed messages create bad impressions, so pay attention to yours. You may not even be aware of the mixed signals you're sending.

Make Eye Contact

As you approach, make eye contact. Shy people find this very difficult. While some cultures consider it bad manners (keep this in mind if you do business internationally), eye contact is absolutely necessary here in the United States to establish your credibility, authority and confidence. It's also necessary for relationship building.

Your Handshake Can Make or Break You

The handshake is vital to first impressions. The quality of your handshake conveys a great deal about you, real or perceived. Remember, 55 percent of first impressions are visual, and that includes the handshake (body language). What does your handshake say about you?

The Limp Handshake

This is an especially important point for women, though it also applies to men. You may have been taught that it is proper behavior to shake hands gently, or maybe you have never been taught how to shake hands at all. In any case, a limp handshake may imply that you are not a decision maker and that you lack confidence in your ability to perform your work or run your business. People want to do business with those who exude confidence. The limp handshake says this person is not confident or capable enough to get the job done. This seriously damages your credibility and authority.

When offered by a woman, it can also be perceived as feminine. But in business, you want people focused on your business ability, not your femininity, which unfortunately can discount you. Interestingly, women may perceive men using a limp handshake as patronizing and sexist—someone that believes women don't belong in the workplace. Such a man, while being friendly and cordial (passive-aggressive behavior) is uncomfortable working with women and often prefers to work with and give his business to men. The way to recognize this person is to pay attention to his conversation with you. Is it flowered with talk about non-business topics or about how great it is to see women in business, or is he interested in learning about *your* business?

There are always exceptions to the above, such as not being taught how to correctly shake hands (both men and women), so don't be too hasty to make judgments. Just make sure your hand-shake is firm and gather more evidence before making final decisions about anyone. Give everyone the benefit of the doubt.

The Killer Handshake

This is generally a male trait, though I've witnessed it with some women as well. When a man uses an overly hard handshake with a woman, it sends a different message than if he did so with another man. Women I've polled told me they interpret killer handshakes from men as well as women as a need to impress, assert domination (the Alpha syndrome), demonstrate masculinity, or cover discom-fort in dealing with women in business. When a man uses a killer handshake with another man, he sends a message of competition, one-upmanship, aggression and dominance. With both genders, the killer handshake makes a negative impression.

Before passing final judgments, though, get to know these people better and determine their business savvy and the positions they hold. In most of my presentations on networking, when we get to this section on the handshake, the novices are genuinely surprised to learn not only the importance of a good handshake but how it's being interpreted.

Is there a difference in handshakes between genders? No. You shake hands the same way with everyone. So how should we shake hands?

The Right Way to Shake Hands

1. Extend your hand and grasp the other person's hand so that the fold between your thumb and forefinger is touching his or her fold.
2. Squeeze firmly, just strong enough to be felt by the other without causing discomfort.
3. Shake up and down once or twice.
4. Release.
5. As you are shaking hands, smile and make eye contact. You're selling your professional brand, and it represents warmth, friendliness, sincerity and authenticity.

Chapter 11

Step 8: Conduct an Engaging Dialogue

You've maneuvered your way to the people you want to meet. You're ready to impress them. What do you say?

HOW TO START A DIALOGUE

Earlier I told you to place your name tag on right side if you shake with your right hand. That's because when you both extend your hands to shake, you can easily see each other's names and company names.

Let's say you spot a woman and decide to approach her. Smile and make eye contact. Extend your hand to shake hers, and using her first name, introduce yourself by your *full name.*

Correct method I: Hi Jeannie, I'm Sheila Savar.

Correct method II: Hi Jeannie, my name is Sheila Savar.

Incorrect method: Hi Jeannie, I'm Sheila.

I can already hear some of you disagreeing with me. In some parts of the country everyone introduces themselves by their first names. But this is a business networking function. Regardless of where you live, when in doubt, formality is better than familiarity (which, if you remember, breeds contempt).

SYNCHRONIZE YOUR STYLES

One of the fastest ways to bond with people and establish rapport is to synchronize by mirroring their behavior—do what they do. If they lean forward as they are speaking to you, you lean in as well. If they sit or stand back to take a sip of their drink as they look you in the eye, pause about 40 to 50 seconds and follow suit. Any sooner and you'll come across as mimicking the other person—a definite no-no!

The theory behind mirroring is that we like people who are like us. If someone is doing what we're doing, we feel he or she is similar to us and share the same mood. It makes us more comfortable. Of course, only mirror positive body language.

Synchronizing makes people comfortable enough with you to focus on your message. To slow talkers, fast talkers create non-productive stress. Slow talkers end up focused on vocals, pitch and body language, not on the message.

If you're a fast talker, get in sync by speaking more slowly to more closely match the quiet person's speed. Smile less (yes, less!), causing your voice pitch to drop. This gains credibility. It's important to note here that a raised pitch, accomplished by smiling, increases approachability. A lowered voice tone increases credibility. Both are important and must be used appropriately.

By getting in sync with slow talkers, you remove their non-productive stress so they can focus on you and your message. If their shyness makes them continue to avoid eye contact, that's fine. You maintain yours as you speak to them (while remaining in sync with them). Eventually, when they feel comfortable with you, they will make eye contact and you'll know you have won them over.

The reverse is also true. Slow talkers put fast talkers to sleep! If you are a slow talker and don't want to lose the attention of fast talker, speed it up. In this example, you, the mild mannered person, approaches the outgoing one. To get and keep the outgoing person's attention, you need to speed it up. Smiling more and raising your voice pitch makes you appear more approachable, putting the fast talker at ease. Now you are both in sync, and the other person can receive your message without getting distracted by a flat tone and lack of animation. To get in sync with another, align with his or her...

- Body language (hand gestures, leaning in, smiling).

- Voice tone and pitch. High pitch equates to approachability, low pitch equates to credibility.

- Verbal communication (conversational speed).

ASK ABOUT HIS OR HER BUSINESS FIRST

Now that you've met, it's time to conduct business. Ask about her company first: "So, Jeannie, what does XYZ Company do?" As she responds, give her your full attention, demonstrated by eye contact. Do not look around the room, wave at people you know, or stare at your watch. You should be focused eye-to-eye on her and your conversation with her. While she is talking, don't interrupt to tell her about your business.

The only time it's appropriate to interrupt is to apply the *80/20 rule*. While the other party is speaking, you listen 80 percent of the time and speak 20 percent of the time. When you speak, it is only to ask her questions about her business. Asking questions shows genuine interest in her work and begins the relationship-building process, because you are having a dialogue rather than listening to her monologue.

Always be prepared to help if you can. A good question to ask is, "Who are your prospects?" You can then be on the lookout for possible prospects for her and perhaps even make a valuable introduction. That question is also a good way to disengage, as we'll discuss shortly. Remember, give before you get. It's a true differentiator.

Your exchange should last a couple of minutes, unless the topic of discussion is of serious value to both of you. After you finish, she should then ask you about your business. Now it's your turn.

YOUR TURN!

Start with your Company Position Statement. As outlined in the Networking Strategy section, you must create a short, 10- to 15-second statement about your company. Memorize it so that it sounds natural and invites people to ask questions. If needed, you can create varying Company Position Statements for different markets and venues, depending on your various business solutions.

Keeping it short increases interest and prompts people to ask questions. Now you have cleverly created an interactive *dialogue*, rather than a canned *monologue,* upon which to base a business relationship with this person. The purpose of networking functions is not to close sales or make deals; its purpose is to make good contacts. So, focus first on building relationships that serve as solid foundations, then follow up for future business opportunities.

HOW TO USE YOUR BUSINESS CARDS

The most important piece of marketing collateral you own is your business card. As discussed in Part III, it is viewed by more people than your website, brochures or other collateral. It should look professional and be well designed, as it is part of your image and professional brand.

How do you exchange cards? Let's revisit the earlier business exchange above. You let the other person speak first. Quite often, when others are finished telling you about their businesses and are about to ask you about yours, they'll offer you their business cards. You can exchange at that time.

But what if the other person doesn't offer a card? What are the right and wrong protocols for handing out business cards?

The Right Way

- After the person has told you about his business, and if he does not offer you his business card, *ask* him for one: "May I get your business card?"

- Before you launch into what you do, you may *ask* for his card: "May I get your business card?"

- Before parting, ask for his card: "It's been a pleasure meeting you. May I ask for one of your business cards?"

- If he does not ask for your card after you have asked for his, *ask* him if you can give him your card before handing it to him. Here you are probably dealing with an inexperienced networker who is more task oriented than socially skilled. He does not mean to be rude. He's simply inexperienced and needs your help. Simply say, "May I give you one of my business cards?"

- When given a business card, always look it over before putting it away. It shows interest. Many people put real effort and feel great pride in designing their cards and appreciate that you give them proper notice before putting them away.

- In some cultures, it's rude to put the business card away without looking at it first. Because most major American cities are very international, it helps to be sensitive and gracious to cultural differences. It makes you *extraordinary!*

- If the card stands out as impressive, unique or eye-catching, let the other person know. People, especially business owners, take pleasure and pride in their business collateral.

The Wrong Way

Never walk around the room, introduce yourself, talk about your business, hand out your business card then move on to the next person without even asking about theirs. Your goal is not to see how many cards you can give away by the end of the evening. You don't want to look like is a used card salesperson!

Another no-no is to first hand someone your business card and then stand there saying nothing, having just been introduced by a third party. It's tacky, very unprofessional, earns you a bad name and is a waste of your time and business cards.

HOW TO DISENGAGE GRACEFULLY

One of the most frequently asked questions I get when I give networking presentations is, "How do I disengage from a person without appearing rude?" When I ask them what they think they should do, many reply that they disengage by stating that they're going to go get something to eat! Let me share two kinder methods that I find very effective.

The Turnover Method

This has nothing to do with food. Earlier I said that the best way to get you over your fear is to help others get over theirs. That means that you approached them, learned about their businesses and asked who their ideal prospects would be.

You realize that you met someone earlier that would benefit from an introduction to this person. So as you escort you new friend over to the third party, you tell him or her about this other beneficial contact and make the introductions. You stay with them until they feel comfortable enough engaging in conversation and then you excuse yourself by saying something like, "I'll leave you two to learn more about each other's businesses."

This is my favorite because I love helping others find the resources they need to become successful. And a great way to ask for referrals is to find them for others first. I truly believe that the way to achieve your success is by helping others achieve theirs.

Don't Want to Prevent You Method

If after five minutes or so, the person you are talking with has no intention of disengaging, and there is little business opportunity to make it worth your while to continue, say something along these lines: "It's been a pleasure getting to know you, but I don't want to keep you from meeting other people."

In both methods you need to conclude with some sort of intention. For example, if you want to follow up to explore potential business opportunities, you complete one of the above disengagement methods with, "I'll follow up with an e-mail tomorrow to schedule a meeting to continue our conversation." If the person is not someone you want to follow up with, end your conversation by saying, "It's been a pleasure meeting you, and I look forward to meeting you at other XYZ networking events."

IS THE NETWORKING PROCESS A ONE SIZE FITS ALL?

There are business functions and occasions where the networking processes described above are inappropriate. If you get seriously involved in a charity or business organization, or you are invited to a business black-tie event, you'll very likely meet senior executives. These are also very expensive functions at several hundred dollars per person. This is another good reason for getting involved with a charity organization. They often show their appreciation for your volunteerism by inviting you to such affairs.

At formal affairs, the networking process described earlier is inappropriate. You will not walk around the room, interject yourself into conversations, speak about your businesses for a few minutes then exchange business cards and promise to follow up before disengaging.

Networking at the senior executive level develops over time. It is more low key and less intense, mostly because these people are already successful and have the luxury to move at a slower pace, developing their relationships over time.

Here the protocol is very different, and the atmosphere is more conservative. Often there is a reception followed by dinner. At a non-profit reception, the non-profit organization's employees should introduce you to their senior executive guests. For example when I was invited by the United Way staff to attend one of their exclusive Alexis de Tocqueville events held at the French Embassy—their way of thanking me for all the volunteer work I'd done—the staff made a point of introducing me to their distinguished Tocqueville members. These are individuals that donate $10,000 and up. As I write this, I'm pleased to announce that today I am the Co-Chair of this great society for the United Way National Capital Area (as well as this year's Campaign Chair).

At these functions, you don't offer your business card or ask for others' unless the conversation warrants it. When engaged in conversation, you will spend more time with each person, but be sensitive to the senior executive's desire to disengage. Remember, because of their senior status they prefer to socialize with their peers. You do not want to monopolize their time.

You can build relationships with these C-Level executives, but it occurs gradually as you work together to support the organization you both serve. Once the relationship is formed, it will be invaluable. So proceed with grace and caution, and follow protocol. If in doubt, observe others or ask your host or hostess.

Once seated at the dinner table, stay there. Speak to the people at your table and get to know them. But again, don't pass out business cards or ask for theirs unless the conversation warrants it. Follow their lead; you are the novice, and they have the experience. Be warm, gracious and friendly. Because they are more senior in position, ask about their work and their interests. Show genuine interest in your conversation and demonstrate your good manners by keeping your eyes focused on them and not wandering about the room trying to identify other important people to connect with later. This is rude and will be noticed.

Don't discuss *your* work unless they ask. In this environment, business is handled gradually and subtly. Jumping into what you do and how they could benefit from your work makes you appear the pushy sales person. Remember, people love to buy but hate to be sold. It could jeopardize your credibility, and you may not be invited to future affairs.

Last, as you are the junior executive, be sensitive to their need to disengage from you. They may want to speak to someone else at the table, or leave the table to approach some of their friends. If you notice their eyes scanning the room, that's a signal that they want to move on. Say, "It's been a pleasure getting to know you, but I don't want to monopolize your time." You will appear to be a class act, and that person will remember you by your graciousness, sensitivity and good manners.

HOW TO MAKE A LASTING IMPRESSION

If you want to stand out and be remembered in a good way, follow these tips:

- Give before you get. Help others achieve their goals and objectives first.

- Remember that the test of good manners is graciously putting up with bad.

- Look for ways to help others with their personal needs as well. This could include the name of your hair stylist, a good doctor, real estate agent, financial advisor or day care center.

- Focus on the person and on developing the relationship. Recognize that you will have different levels of relationships. You won't have time to cultivate relationships with everyone you meet, so create a strong diversified inner circle and develop those relationships attentively.

- Show genuine interest and concern for another.

- Be authentic.

- Smile!

- Show warmth and always wear your positive attitude everywhere you go. You'll become known for it.

- Take the time to compliment people and make their day. Most people are quick to criticize but slow to compliment. You stand out when you notice something special about someone and take the time to acknowledge it. You will really make their day and earn their loyalty.

- Honor every commitment you make, regardless of the customer's size or importance in monetary terms.

- Be extraordinary!

For an additional confidence boost, review the Networking Do's and Don'ts in the Appendix just before leaving your car to attend a networking event.

Part IV Highlights

- Always have enough business cards with you at all times. Leave a box in the car if you must. Never attend a networking function without them.

- Image matters, so dress for success. If your income is limited, go to retail outlets and purchase a few quality clothes. Buy when there's a sale. Then buy basic mix and match items to create your wardrobe for work. Your professional brand must be carried over into your work, not restricted to just networking functions. If you desire to move up the corporate ladder: *Dress for the job you want, not for the job you have!*

- Create your positive attitude while still in the car. Look in the rear view mirror and keep smiling until you burst out laughing. Set goals to help you get through the networking event on those days when you are not in the mood to attend but know you must.

- First impressions are lasting impressions. How you enter the room says everything about you. Leading authorities claim your body language and the way you walk and stand indicate your level of confidence and forms 80 percent of their first impression of you!

- Exude confidence to get noticed and gain immediate credibility.

- Enter with a smile, warmth and authenticity. Be friendly to everyone you meet. Thank the people at the registration booth for their good work as you collect your badge.

- As you enter the networking reception, start by approaching the singles first. It's easier on you, and they will really appreciate your approach. Avoid couples and large groups until you feel like a networking pro.

- When greeting a fellow networker, smile and shake hands. Ask about his or her business first. Then apply the 80/20 rule—give your full attention 80 percent of the time, speaking only 20 percent of the time. When you do speak, ask questions about the other person's business. Ask about his or her "ideal prospects" so you can help make connections either during or after the networking event.

- Before talking about your business, ask for the other person's business card if it's not already offered. Look at it before putting it away. If he or she doesn't ask for yours, ask if you can give them your card as well before handing it over.

- Introduce your business by using your memorized Company Position Statement. It needs to be short and sound natural to create interest and get the other person to ask questions. This creates a dialogue, rather than a boring monologue, and helps to build the relationship.

- After about five minutes, disengage gracefully using one of two methods. Introduce the person to someone they may want to meet, such as a potential prospect, or state that you do not want to monopolize their time and prevent them from meeting others. Either way, you are demonstrating consideration for the other person's time, not yours, and you will make a favorable impression.

- Networking functions are not the right venue for *closing business*. They're for *initiating business* by identifying prospects. Once identified, the sales process continues after the event when you follow up with your prospects to ask for a meeting.

- How you conduct yourself at an event depends on the event and the attendees. If you are invited to a C-level affair (usually black-tie), remember to follow the rules outlined earlier; the standard networking protocol does not apply here.

- To give yourself added confidence, review the networking do's and don't before leaving your car.

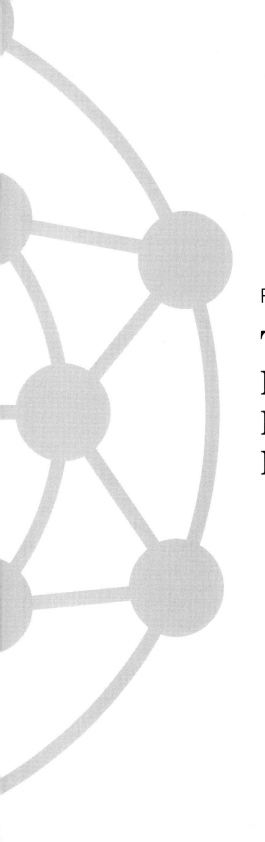

PART V

The Networking Follow-Up Process

Chapter 12
After the Networking Event

You did it—you lived through your ordeal, and you did a splendid job! Hopefully you had a pretty good time and made a few good contacts. Now its time to rate the contacts while the evening and the contacts are fresh in your mind.

RATE THE BUSINESS CARDS YOU COLLECTED

It's best to do this next exercise while you're still in the car, while the network experience is fresh. Have a pen handy. Let's say you spoke with ten people and collected their business cards. Not all are prospects. Not all are equally important. But all are worth storing and saving as part of your network, because you never know when one comes in handy (refer back to my Introduction if you forgot).

You need to create a rating system. It can be anything you want it to be, based on your particular job. For example, you create a rating system of A-List, B-List and C-List business cards (kind of like Hollywood celebrities!), and attach values to each.

A-List cards are *strong leads*. These are good prospects—people that have shared a *goal, objective, challenge or need* that can be addressed and resolved with a business solution your company provides. These are strong sales opportunities. So on the back of these cards, write an A.

A B-List card may be a person that sells in your same vertical (industry) or horizontal (small, middle or large sized companies) market. This contact can become an alliance or teaming partner, or a part of your virtual sales team. Both can create impressive revenue generating opportunities. To build an effective virtual sales team, one that is more likely to bring you leads, offer incentives, such as:

- Pay a flat referral fee for any referrals that result in a sale.

- Pay a percentage of the sales quote value on any referrals that close.

- Agree to a mutual exchange of leads. This is especially necessary when dealing with sales reps from major companies. They are not permitted to accept monetary incentives for referrals.

In the above scenarios, you create exponential sales growth through the use of alliances, teaming partners and virtual sales teams.

Your C-List cards may be potential provider-partners, vendors, or contacts of no immediate value.

You decide how to rate your cards. You do not have to limit them to three categories, but here is what you must do:

1. Evaluate your performance.

2. Store all business cards physically and electronically by industry (more on this in the next section).

EVALUATE YOUR PERFORMANCE

The only way to improve your performance is to consistently evaluate it. To succeed in business you should always be striving for excellence in everything you do, and that includes your networking skills. A few moments when you're back in your car is the perfect time to evaluate your networking performance. If you're too exhausted, please do it the very next day.

Reading this book is just the first step. Without practicing and then evaluating what you've learned, you gain nothing. If you're serious about building a powerful network that will serve you and your business for a lifetime, you'll "practice, practice, practice" until you are master of your game. Is my motivational presentation (i.e. guilt trip) working?

To help you to evaluate your performance, I've included the Networking Performance Analysis Form that I hand out to students taking my networking seminars and workshops. Spend a few moments reviewing it then we'll discuss each section in detail. Make copies of the form to keep in your car; you'll be completing one after each networking event until you are master of your networking game. Did I say that already? Oh well, it bears repeating!

Networking Performance Analysis Form

Event Organization: _____ Date: _____

Event Venue: _____ RONI: High_____ Low: _____

Attendees: _____

What I did well and want to develop:

   1._____

   2._____

   3._____

What I'd like to improve:

   1._____

   2._____

   3._____

My action plan:

   1._____

   2._____

   3._____

Let's examine each part of the performance form so you will feel comfortable completing it after a networking event.

Event Organization: Jot down the name of the organization that hosted the event.

Date: Write in the date of the event.

Event Venue: Where was the event held? Name the venue, city and even state if applicable. This helps you remember events more easily.

RONI (Return on Networking Investment): Rate the event as either having a high value or a low value. This is part of your networking strategy and helps you determine which events to continue attending and which to drop.

Attendees: Who were the primary attendees? Were the attendees the types of businesspeople you had hoped to meet? This is a good way to evaluate a particular event for future reference.

What I did well: List three things that you felt you did well. If this is your first time, be generous with your praise. Being too hard on yourself will only deflate your confidence and prevent you from wanting to try again.

What I'd like to improve: List three things that you were not comfortable performing and would like to improve upon. Again, this is not designed to be judgmental and break your spirit. This is an exercise for improvement as you strive for networking excellence (and you will achieve it!).

My action plan: For each of the items you listed above, list your improvement strategy. For example, when you entered the networking reception, you didn't use that all important smile. Instead you went to the buffet and began eating, hoping no one would notice you, or better yet, someone would notice and rescue you. Here you write that next time, you will exude confidence, walk in with a smile, look for the people standing along the wall and begin a conversation with them. The Networking Performance Analysis Form does several good things for you. It:

- Tracks the networking events you attend.

- Creates a networking profile (helping you to remember the event).

- Provides valuable information about the event and the attendees.

- Helps you to improve your performance.

Keep your evaluations in the car and review your last performance form before entering the next networking event. That's how you'll continue to improve.

FOLLOW UP THE NEXT DAY

The day after a networking function, you should have several business cards. If you rated them while you were still in the car, well done! If not, do it now. What do you do next? There are several follow-up tasks that will help you build a powerful network. How well you do them determines the quality of your network and the power and influence you will one day be known to have. Within the first 24 hours, contact each person whose business card you received and send an e-mail that is appropriate based on your rating system.

A-List Cards

Send an e-mail. You can also call, and if they are unavailable, leave a voice mail message requesting a meeting and letting them know that you'll also be following up with an e-mail. In the e-mail indicate that it was a pleasure meeting them, and say something to jog their memory about you and why you are writing. Then request a meeting by asking them to send you a couple of their available dates over the next couple of weeks. This makes you look equally busy. I prefer e-mail contact as more often than not a phone call usually gets voice mail. If you leave a message asking him to return the call, he will probably forget, despite his best intentions. E-mails are less intrusive, stay in people's in-boxes until addressed or deleted, and people can respond at their convenience.

Remember that the A-List people are hot prospects where both parties are interested in a follow-up business meeting. These people should be as interested to hear from you as you are to contact them. I am rarely disappointed by lack of a response. But should this happen, I simply follow up with a call. After they apologize for forgetting, we schedule an appointment. I prefer to invite A-List people to lunch at my business club rather than go to their office. It gives me the home court advantage.

Does this sound way too time-consuming? After all, you have a stack of business cards, and if you spend your time sending an e-mail to each person, your day is shot. Don't despair! I have a sure-fire shortcut for you. Write one e-mail and send it to the first A-List person. Copy and paste it to the second A-List person's e-mail. Then just tweak it to make it appropriate for them. Continue doing this until you've sent e-mails to all your A-List contacts.

B-List Cards

Again within 24 hours, contact B-List people using the same method as described above. Invite them for coffee to discuss how the two of you can work together to expand business opportunity between your companies. Create another e-mail template as you did for the A-List.

C-List Cards

Within 24 hours, send an e-mail expressing how much you enjoyed meeting them and that you look forward to seeing them again at other similar functions. Again, use an e-mail template.

For all lists, if you are scheduling meetings, don't request specific dates or use sleazy, insincere, old-school sales tactics ("I'm going to be in your area next Monday. Can we meet?") It can easily backfire. If the person is not available on Monday, what then? Today's buyers are far too sophisticated and will be turned off by such inauthentic sales tactics. Nothing is more refreshing than an honest and sincere approach. Complete these tasks as you conduct your business—with authenticity and integrity. Never forget that you are a partner, not a vendor.

IS THERE VALUE TO PEOPLE I MEET THAT ARE NOT PROSPECTS?

Yes. There is value to everyone you meet, even your C-List (not to be confused with C-level) contacts, because:

- They may know someone who is a prospect for you.
- They may change jobs and be in a position to retain your services.
- They can say good things about you to mutual prospects and clients.
- They may start their own venture and need your services in the future.
- They may be an excellent information resource in your future.

Not everyone has a naturally outgoing personality. You may be shy and far more comfortable working on a project than being around people. I'm not asking you to be what you are not. That would be inauthentic. Just follow the networking process I've outlined for you in this section, but make it your own special, unique brand. If you're shy and quiet, that's fine. Just remember to be polite and courteous and show interest in the other person's business when it's his or her turn to speak. Most importantly, learn to smile more often. Smiling may not come naturally to task-oriented people but it's

critical for networking success because it makes you approachable—
a requirement at networking functions! Practice, practice, practice
until its second nature to you.

Chapter 13
How to Organize Your Contacts

Now that you have sent the obligatory e-mails and made the anticipatory appointments, what do you do with the business cards you've gathered? Is there any value to them, or should you throw them out? If you answer that you should throw them out, bite your tongue!

Those business cards are the building blocks of your powerful and impressive network. But before we discuss how to maximize on Return on Networking Investment (RONI), we have to discuss how you plan to store your business cards. You need to create two types of storage systems: physical and electronic.

PHYSICAL STORAGE

I store other people's business cards in the boxes in which my business cards were delivered. As I use mine up, I have space for the new business cards that I've collected. But you don't want to randomly throw them into the box. On the back of each card:

1. Rate the opportunity (A, B, C).

2. Note the networking function, venue and date.

3. Note the industry.

You're already familiar with #1 above, but what about #2 and #3? By jotting down the networking function (e.g., XYZ Chamber of Commerce), venue (the ABC Hotel in New York City) and date, I'm creating a history of where I met this person. If they ever call me, and I don't remember them, I can appear to remember by referencing the information I've stored. Is that insincere? I don't think so. People want to be remembered. It's far kinder to refer to your notes than to tell them you don't remember meeting them. Which would *you* prefer?

The networking function information on the backs of the business cards, as well as your Networking Performance Evaluation Forms helps to determine your RONI. If after six months you've attended 8 to 10 functions sponsored by the XYZ Chamber of Commerce, and have not received a single prospect, it's time to drop them from your list of networking organizations. Otherwise you're wasting your time and your money.

The last item (#3) to note on the back of the business card is the company's industry. Why? If you answered because it's easier to remember that person by their industry than by either their personal name or company name, you get a gold star!

Let's imagine a contact of yours asks if you know any financial advisors. Because you have created a process for managing your contacts, you can easily obtain that information for this contact. What do you suppose this person is thinking about you? He or she is probably wondering if there's anyone you *don't* know. That's how you earn a reputation of being a power person.

ELECTRONIC STORAGE: CONTACT MANAGEMENT SYSTEMS

A physical storage device is one of two systems you need for tracking your contacts. The other is an electronic storage device, into which you'll transfer all your card information. You need both of these systems right from the beginning. Don't wait until your business cards are all over your desk or office to start thinking about organizing them. You'll never get around to it. Plus you cannot conduct business efficiently and effectively, or provide exceptional customer experiences, without some form of contact management software. I prefer ACT! software and have been using it for years. It's inexpensive, user-friendly, customizable and very versatile.

An electronic database (ACT! or other similar contact management software) gives you the flexibility to do lookups, conduct searches and queries, group contacts by geographical location, schedule activities, write notes, keep a history and audit of each contact and so on. Electronic storage devices are far more useful and valuable to you than physical devices and processes. But still keep the physical business card. I don't believe in throwing them away. What if your system crashes and you didn't do a backup? You'll need your cards to rebuild your database.

You are probably currently using Microsoft Office software and have either Microsoft Outlook or Microsoft Outlook Express along with it. You also want to get the business card information into one of those programs for storage and e-mailing purposes.

If you attend many networking functions, you're going to have a lot of business cards to input. I highly recommend that you invest in a business card scanner. They're worth the couple of hundred dollars it will cost you. I use CardScan by Corex. It comes with easy-to-use software, and once you've scanned your cards, you can transfer them to several of the more popular contact management programs.

Once I scan my business cards and create the contact lists, I upload them into Microsoft Outlook software (for e-mailing purposes) and into my ACT! Database. It has been my "administrative assistant" since 1990 and without it I would not be able to provide my clients with those exceptional customer experiences for which Savar & Associates is known. For more information on this software, go to www.act.com. They offer a 30-day free trial, and I like that!

I'm going to assume that you have direct contact with your clients. In order to grow your business, it's not enough to just get new customers. You must transform them into loyal clients in order to get their repeat business. *Loyal* clients don't leave you for a better price from your competitor, *satisfied* customers do.

So how do you create client loyalty? By having automated processes in place to support your clients so that promises made become honored commitments. Forgetting to follow up can and will cost you your credibility and eventually your customer. You will also use your database as a powerful networking tool. It contains information that is valuable to you and to others in the business community. As you share that information, you earn a reputation. Remember, information is powerful. When you have access to information that people want, you become a power person.

Part V Highlights

- Back in the car while your memory is still fresh, turn the business cards over and rate each one using the rating system you created.

- Also while in the car, review your performance. Complete a Performance Analysis Form. Leave it in the car so you can review it before going into your next networking event. It will act as a quick refresher.

- The next day, follow up with each person you met by sending an e-mail. If you are scheduling appointments with A-List people, you may call, but still follow up with e-mails. This gives the option of either returning your call or your e-mail.

- As you become a networking expert, remember that the most important ingredients are warmth, honesty, sincerity and authenticity. That's how you want to be known. Don't come across as a mechanical person just going through the motions. I've known people like this, and even as they are smiling, I feel nothing behind that smile.

- Begin developing relationships with those you want as part of your inner circle. Do it immediately, not when you need a favor. By then it's too late to make such requests.

- You must have both physical and electronic storage methods for your business cards. Your business success is based on having the means to access data easily and efficiently. That definitely includes your contact data, especially your prospects and clients. Your hard networking efforts will reap little reward without such systems.

- There is value in storing your business cards physically by industry rather than alphabetically. It's easier to remember the industry than the contact or company name.

- It's important to scan or key all business card data into an electronic database system that gives you data manipulation flexibility. A sound technological infrastructure and accompanying software programs help you manage and deliver commitments you make to your clients earning you an excellent reputation and your clients' loyalty. It also provides access to vital business information that you or others in your network may need. You become known as a well connected power person!

PART VI

Return on Networking Investment (RONI)

Chapter 14

How to Maximize Your Return on Networking Investment (RONI)

The better connected you are, the more power you have, and the more marketable you become. Today we live in a global economy where the world is now *flat*. How can we expand our contact base so that it grows exponentially and has worldwide capabilities? Why would we want to?

I live in the Washington, D. C. area, and I love its international flavor and appeal. Today it's as easy to call my friend a few miles away as it is to call another friend in Beijing, China. Because so many businesspeople conduct business internationally, we want contacts within our network to have global capabilities. That adds more value for us and for others looking to us for resources.

Recently I received an e-mail from someone I met while I was visiting a company he worked for in Bangalore, India in 2001. He called to say he was here in my area and asked to meet for coffee. He told me he had left that company in India and formed a new one with three partners. When I asked him how he had gotten my e-mail address (I was with another company when I had visited India), he told me that my name was one of two "must meet" people his local U.S. contact had given him. Coincidentally, the other contact and I also know each other!

ONLINE CONTACT SYSTEMS

To connect globally, you need to be able to store your contact information on the Internet as well. You need a program that is easy to use, keeps you connected and helps to expand your business contacts exponentially. Here are a couple of the most popular programs on the World Wide Web. Both are free for basic usage, and they charge a small monthly fee for their expanded services.

LinkedIn

This Internet based program allows you to store your contact information and to invite people to become a part of your virtual network. You can invite every business card contact or just select contacts. On the receiving end, you may elect to decline an invitation from someone that you do not feel shares your business principles and ethics.

LinkedIn enables you to post your contact information, information about your business and so forth. The beauty of this system is that it can be accessed worldwide via the Internet.

Your network needs to grow over the years so that it becomes more and more useful to you and to others. Today's student peers and friends can be tomorrow's CEOs! Here are some of the great features of LinkedIn:

- It allows you to invite people into your network, so each contact on a business card can become someone you choose to invite into your network.

- If you are changing jobs or relocating, imagine the hassle of having to contact everyone you know to give them your new information. With LinkedIn you send it out once, and everyone in your network receives the information and updates theirs to include your newest contact information.

- You can search for a job, look for a specific employee, or ask for special assistance on a particular problem. It will go out to your network, and someone among them should be able to help.

- It grows exponentially, making your network that much more powerful. Let's say you invite 10 people to join your network and eight accept. Each of those eight has networks of their own. When you combine their networks with yours, can you see its exponential growth and the power you are creating?

To learn more, please visit their website at www.linkedin.com.

Plaxo

This program's core service is free to everyone who joins. You update your information, your contacts update theirs, and everyone stays in touch. You can download toolbars to access a single, up-to-date address book across all of the applications you use. Here are some benefits:

- Update your address book when friends and business associates change their contact information.

- Update contacts' address books when your contact information changes.

- Synchronize your contacts, calendars, tasks, and notes across Plaxo's applications.

- Get reminded of a contact's birthday just a few days before.

- Receive an alert whenever a contact's information has changed.

For more information on Plaxo, visit their website at www.plaxo.com.

Whichever service you choose, you are growing your network exponentially and globally. You can make all kinds of requests through these programs. Let's say your company is opening an office in Mumbai, India, and you need twenty talented people for various positions. You can post that request right in Plaxo or LinkedIn and your contacts go to work for you. Think of the time and cost savings. How powerful is that!

BUILD RELATIONSHIPS WITH YOUR PROSPECTS

You will meet hundreds if not thousands of people through your networking efforts. It's not possible or practical to develop relationships . with everyone you meet, so you must be strategic in your relationship building approach.

You will have different circles of contacts. Your inner circle should consist of at least your clients, prospective clients, lead exchange partners, provider-partners, and some well connected people that provide win-win business opportunities.

These are the people with whom you need to develop relationships. This is a gradual process, not an overnight one. You cultivate and nurture these relationships as you would friendships. These are the people you can call on when you need a favor and vice versa.

But what about all the rest of the people you meet? How do you stay connected to them so they don't forget you? Or should you even bother? Yes, you should stay connected to everyone you meet, because you never know when one may eventually become a prospect in need of your service. You want them to remember you and seek you out.

STAY IN FRONT OF YOUR CONTACTS

In order to capitalize on your networking investment, you must stay connected to your network so they don't forget you. Earlier I said that the average person needs seven interactions with another in order to be remembered. This also applies in sales. Most salespeople fail because they give up too soon—after two or three attempts, when the average buyer needs 5 to 7 interactions before making a final buying decision. Many of the contacts you meet through networking events may not need your services today, but they might tomorrow or a year from now. You must stay in touch with them in order to be remembered.

If you've made a great impression on a contact a year ago but didn't stay in touch with her, how will she reach you now that she has a need for your services? What will she most likely do? If she's a networker, she's probably met several companies similar to yours, and she'll call the most recent one—the one she remembers.

If she's not a regular networker, chances are she never stored your information, or she lost your card and can't remember how to reach you. So she'll do what many less sophisticated people do: she'll do an online search for local providers. Either way, you've just lost a great prospecting opportunity.

So how do you avoid this? Stay in touch with your contacts on a regular basis—at least every two to three months. You can do this in a variety of ways (feel free to get creative here) such as:

- Create and send quarterly eZines containing information valuable to your contacts.

- Send press releases and announcements about your business.

- Host an informative breakfast or luncheon and speak about topics your company provides and that are of relevance to your audience. Do not promote or sell your products or service during the event; that is considered to be in poor taste. But do have literature and information for people to take. You can always follow up after the event.

- If you come across information a particular person may want, email it or clip it and send it with a handwritten note.

- Find out your contact's birthday and send a card (Plaxo programs automatically alert you of a contact's birthday and they offer some free electronic birthday cards).

- If you read about a decision maker's recent promotion, send a note of congratulations (whether you know her or not). After a couple of weeks, follow up with a request for a meeting.

You might be wondering, "Sure, it's easy to send a card, but how do I go about creating a professional press release, invitation or quarterly eZine, especially if I'm not creatively or technologically inclined?"

A very affordable and user-friendly, web-based solution is a product called Constant Contact. This online program enables everyone, even the technologically challenged, to create affordable, professional-looking e-mail campaigns, invitations, postcards and eZines that help you stay connected with your contact database which is everyone in your network. The Constant Contact program also allows you to group your contacts so you can send special mailers to specific groups, organizations, clients etc. For more information on this product, visit www.constantcontact.com. They offer a 60-day free trial.

BUILD A VIRTUAL SALES TEAM

Business opportunities present themselves in a variety of ways. You have to be open and creative to recognize one. You may attend a function and not meet a prospect, but instead meet a salesperson or small business owner that calls on your targeted market of prospects. This can be great if you take advantage of the situation and create a win-win by building your virtual sales team.

Here virtual means that they are not your employees, but they do call on the same prospect base offering different or complementary business solutions. For example, they may call on human resources departments because they offer an HR software program. You call on HR departments to provide temporary and permanent staffing services.

Remember when I told you that it's sometimes okay to attend less expensive networking functions where you're more likely to meet other sales representatives rather than decision makers? Well here is where it pays off. If you are in a position to do so, offer your virtual sales team a referral fee for every warm lead they bring you (as we discussed in Part II).

A warm lead can be an introduction through e-mail or an in-person introduction that your virtual sales representative coordinates between you and the prospective buyer. The referral fee can either be a percentage of sales (e.g., five percent of the quoted amount) or a flat fee based on the size of the sale. The terms are negotiable between you and your virtual representative.

A virtual sales team can increase revenue almost effortlessly. You should reciprocate this process, if your company's rules allow it or if you are the owner. If your company does not allow you to accept payment, you can simply agree to exchange leads as you call on the same prospect base.

FORM TEAMING ALLIANCES

Sometimes you may find yourself faced with a contract larger than your small business can handle. You may not have sufficient human and financial resources to respond and deliver in accordance to the requirements. But you may be able to handle it with some help and without having to expand your human and technological infrastructure. An effective solution is a teaming alliance.

With an alliance partner, you don't need to borrow money or hire more people. You become the prime contractor, and your alliance partner is the subcontractor (even if they are considerably larger than your company). This strategy is used quite often when government agencies set aside certain contracts for small minority-owned businesses.

DEVELOP PROVIDER-PARTNER RELATIONSHIPS

We go to networking functions to find new business, but there will be many times when we are the buyers and need work performed for us. Wouldn't you rather buy from someone either within or referred by your network? People that know you or are referred to you have an even greater vested interest in doing a good job. And they have a lot more to lose if they do a bad job, especially if you are well connected in the business community. They will end up with an unhappy client (you) who will let the referred party know about it. They can lose their reputation, so they're highly motivated to keep you happy.

Once you start networking, you quickly realize how small the business community really is. You cannot afford to make someone unhappy. It's too high a price to pay and can seriously damage your business. So always do a great job!

EXCHANGE SERVICES

This is another of the many advantages of attending networking functions. It is not uncommon to meet people who have immediate needs for your service and you for theirs. Your prices may be close enough for you to become *alliance partners*—businesses that exchange services and support and promote each other's services. It's a true win-win scenario.

One of my alliance partners and I have exchanged many referrals. After we formed our partnership, my clients started commenting on the exceptional courtesy and efficiency of my receptionists. They are, actually, my alliance partner's receptionists. You see, part of our exchange agreement is that I provide monthly customer care training to his staff in exchange for his company's services.

Part VI Highlights

- Networking functions are often places where relationships begin. You may meet prospects or contacts that can eventually become prospects.

- Develop relationships with those offering mutual value to your organizations. When a favor is needed, you can call on your inner circle of relationships to help and vice versa. Don't wait to build the relationship when you need the favor. By then it's too late.

- To ensure that you are remembered, stay in front of all your contacts. Be creative and use a variety of approaches to stay connected. Some ideas include e-mails and phone calls, invitations to share a meal or coffee, or sending interesting articles and eZines. By staying in touch with your network, they will contact you and not your competitor when they need your services.

- Companies large and small are doing business globally, thanks to today's technological advances. Being globally connected is critical to your business growth and continued success. Stay connected by using appropriate web-based software as another way to keep in touch with your network and allow your contacts to stay in touch with you.

- Building a virtual sales team can generate serious revenue for your business. Motivate your sales team with monetary incentives for each referral that results in a close. Offer reciprocity where applicable.

- While building your virtual sales team, you can expand revenue exponentially by encouraging team members to offer the same monetary incentives to their network. This way, everybody wins.

- Teaming alliances play an important role in increasing revenues. When a business opportunity presents itself that your company's resources alone cannot fulfill, having contacts within your network that you trust to form teaming alliances allows you to respond to an opportunity that you would otherwise have had to bypass.

- Using your network when you need to secure a new service provider is working efficiently and productively. The referrals you get through your contacts lower the risk associated with making a poor selection. This ensures better quality and almost immediate results. That translates to dollars and time saved!

- Exchanging services can be a mutually advantageous and profitable venture. In such relationships, you have the added bonus of promoting each other's businesses and referring business to each other.

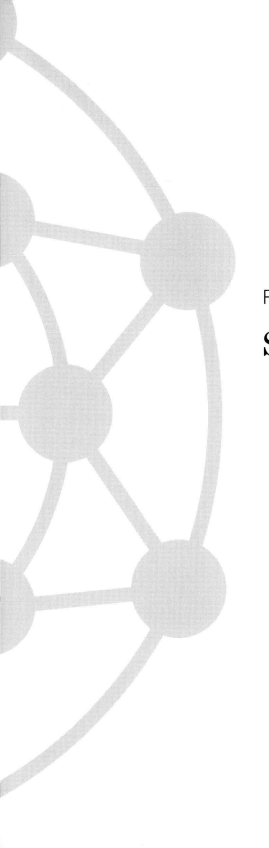

PART VII

Summary

Chapter 15
Networking in a Nutshell

B y now you should know that the primary objective most people have for attending networking functions is to find prospects and secure business (sales). But we have also discussed at length a host of secondary benefits to networking and creating a powerful network of contacts.

We started by learning how to develop the right networking strategy to meet your goals and objectives. You should now know that you need it to achieve your goals and objectives more quickly, efficiently and economically. You create your networking strategy by:

1. Setting your annual revenue (sales) goals.

2. Targeting your market segment by attending networking functions where you are most likely to meet decision making prospects (saving time and money).

3. Creating an interesting Company Position Statement that explains your business and engages others in a dialogue that builds relationships (rather than a monologue that creates boredom and loss of attention).

4. Joining selected industry or association committees and evaluating results to ensure your RONI.

5. Getting involved with charity organizations as an effective way to meet senior executives while giving back to your community.

Having developed your solid networking strategy, we moved on to learn how to network effectively at events, again to maximize your RONI. Here we focused on the *networking process* and the steps to take to ensure a successful networking outcome:

1. Take plenty of business cards.

2. Dress for success.

3. Prepare for the networking function.

4. Determine whether to attend with a business associate or go alone.

5. Know what to do when entering the networking venue.

6. Handle food and drinks appropriately.

7. Know how to conduct yourself once inside the networking reception.

8. Gracefully engage and disengage with people you meet.

9. Begin rating the business cards and complete your Performance Evaluation Form once you return to your car (before you leave).

10. Within 24 hours, contact everyone you met by e-mail. You may also call your A-List prospects.

Next we discussed how to physically and electronically store all of the business cards you collected. We concluded with a number of ways to benefit from business alliances and staying connected to your contacts so that you will be remembered as well as easily reached when someone needs your services:

1. Get globally connected (LinkedIn or Plaxo programs).

2. Create virtual sales teams and referral programs.

3. Stay in front of your contacts (e.g., through eZines).

4. Develop important relationships early on—before you need a favor.

5. Create teaming alliances.

6. Exchange services.

With this information, you are well on your way to being an impressive networker who stands out above the crowd!

REPETITION CREATES EXCELLENCE

It's important that you consistently work at improving your networking skills until they become second nature to you. The more comfortable you are with networking, the more comfortable people will feel in your presence. You will naturally generate warmth and authenticity and attract people to you like a magnet.

Remember, we do business with people we like, and we like people that are similar to us. That makes us feel comfortable.

Chapter 16

A Few True Stories to Illustrate the Value of Networking

Have you heard the expression that luck is simply opportunity meeting preparedness? If we go prepared, networking is the venue for the opportunities we seek. Here are a few examples—some mine while some are shared by people in my network—that illustrate the power of networking.

UNEXPECTED FACE-TO-FACE
WITH CEO RESULTS IN MAJOR SALE

In December 2005 I joined an online, culturally diverse organization called DiversityBusiness.com. It offers a membership database. I searched through it and identified all the companies in my area, and I sent holiday cards to each of the local companies. My cards are bordered with flags of different nations. I hoped that would stand out, especially to companies that were into cultural diversity.

One of the companies especially grabbed my interest because of its unique name—SiloSmashers—and because it was a woman-owned business. I sent Angela Drummond, SiloSmashers founder and CEO, a card. I never heard back, nor did I expect to. In February my alma mater, George Mason University, sponsored a full day business and venture capital boot camp for small business owners. They are big on networking in our community. I received the e-mail invitation and reviewed the full day agenda. Remember what I said about luck earlier? Well, guess who the keynote speaker was? None other than Angela Drummond; the CEO of SiloSmashers who I had wanted to meet.

I didn't want to stay the full day. But because I wanted to hear Angela's keynote presentation, I arrived fifteen minutes before lunch. While waiting for the doors to the lunch reception area to open, a vivacious, attractive, warm and authentic woman walked up to me. I liked her instantly; she reminded me of me! This was Angela Drummond. I started laughing and told her about how I had heard of her and SiloSmashers. I had come specifically to hear her speak, and here she was standing in front of me. It turned out we were both members of the Tower Club, our business club.

We had lunch together and hit it off immediately. We have so much in common, it was spooky. Since Angela had told me that she was looking for training, I went to SiloSmashers to meet with their President and their COO to close one of my biggest sales last year.

And the best part is that we have become friends. Not just Angela and I, but the President and the COO, as well! SiloSmashers is among my favorite clients because they share my values of honesty and integrity and my passion for providing their clients with exceptional customer experiences.

EXECUTIVE SEEKING CAREER CHANGE
LANDS EXECUTIVE VICE PRESIDENT POSITION

A Senior Vice President of a technology company told me that she got her current job because she and her current CEO met on the dance floor! Beth Miller-Herholtz and her husband, Steve, are enthusiastic dancers. They met Tom and Cindy DeWitt through one of their dance classes and became friends. Soon they were often doing things together as couples—traveling, sharing gourmet dinner parties, and, of course, dancing. It was clear that a common set of values and creativity existed between them. So when Beth confided in Cindy one day that she wanted a career change, Cindy suggested that she consider the company that Tom founded and was growing. After a quick interview, Tom hired her as Vice President of Corporate Development for SNVC (www.snvc.com), a small systems integrator based in Fairfax, Virginia! That's the power of networking, and it can happen anywhere, anytime with anyone.

UNEMPLOYED ATTORNEY RE-ENTERS THE WORKFORCE AND LANDS DREAM JOB!

A couple of years ago a friend of mine relocated to the Washington, D.C. area. Katherine had run a successful law practice representing corporate clients. An earlier business opportunity for her husband had resulted in a relocation that prevented Katherine from practicing law for three years.

At age fifty three, she was concerned. She wanted to reenter the workplace initially as a part-time corporate attorney, though she had never worked in corporate. She sought the help of a professional recruiter that specialized in legal placements.

This is what he told her: "You are too old, haven't worked in three years, and have no experience working as a corporate attorney." Besides that, he added, *"There are no* corporate attorney positions available in the Washington, D.C. metro area." She was completely demoralized. I was livid—clearly, he was anything but qualified!

I encouraged her to attend a networking event with me to boost her confidence. At the networking reception she engaged in conversation with a senior corporate counsel from a large multi-national corporation. They got along well and when Katherine shared her employment objectives, she was invited to interview for a position that was an ideal match. Needless to say, Katherine got the job!

The moral of this story is to never listen to anyone that speaks in generalizations or attempts to discourage you from pursuing your objectives. Instead, strategically select and attend networking venues where you will most likely meet the people that can help you fulfill your needs.

Go where your prospects go, and remember to wear your confidence and your positive attitude!

A HAND UP FOR THE UNITED WAY AND SAVAR & ASSOCIATES!

I have been volunteering for the United Way National Capital Area for almost three years now. I serve on several committees in a variety of roles. The more involved I become, the greater their appreciation. Since they cannot show their appreciation monetarily, they recently compensated by inviting me to attend the very prestigious Alexis de Tocqueville Society event at the French Embassy. To be included in this event you have to be an individual donor giving at the $10,000 or greater level. I did not qualify at that time, but thanks to my volunteerism and this wonderful group's appreciation I received an invitation anyway.

There I met some very senior executives. The higher the volunteer position you accept, the more visibility you have within the organization's membership and the more likely that your fellow volunteers are more senior level executives (i.e. decision makers). As I write this book, I am now a member and co-chair of the Alexis de Tocqueville society for the upcoming year. This is how I had the privilege of meeting John Derrick, former Chair of the Alexis de Tocqueville society and former CEO and Chair of Pepco. That is how I got his endorsement for my book.

That is the power of getting involved with the right charities and organizations. It really makes a big difference in elevating your business circle and your status while you serve your community and gain tremendous satisfaction from knowing you are making a difference in the lives of others.

Chapter 17
Conclusion

It has been a pleasure and an honor to write this book for you. My goal is to help you to achieve business and personal success faster, more efficiently and more affordably.

I want to leave you with some final thoughts on the importance of creating your network and the impact it has on your success:

- Your network helps you work more productively and efficiently. That means it helps you *make* and *save money* more easily.

- As you turn to your network to quickly gain access to prospects, referrals and teaming alliances, your productivity increases and you make money.

- When you turn to your network and access needed service providers, key new hires or a host of other needed products and services, you work more effectively and efficiently, save your company money, reduce the risk of costly mistakes and increase your confidence in making the right selection.

- When you find a mentor or two, you will be fortunate enough to have the wisdom of experienced, successful people who can provide career and business guidance and support to ensure your business growth and success.

- Your network will contain very senior level people, because you joined committees of charities near and dear to you. There you have the best chance of meeting the level of executives most of us are very unlikely to meet without getting connected.

- Your network jump starts your career and your business because you have more immediate access to people who can provide you with the resources you need to succeed. Remember it's all about relationships. If people like you, they'll help you. The best way to ask for help is to be the one that helps first.

- We train salespeople to negotiate with a "get before you give" mentality. In networking the reverse applies: give before you get. Become known for being a caring, authentic and helpful person, and your reputation will grow right alongside your business!

- Start building your important relationships before you need to ask a favor.

- Help everyone whenever possible. Don't categorize by title, such as "competitor" or "CEO." Treat everyone like a friend and a CEO and offer your help. While others may believe in business scarcity and fear they won't get a slice of the proverbial pie, you believe in abundance and know that in order to get more business, all you have to do is just bake a bigger pie!

- Information is power. When you are known to be well connected, you earn the respect of your business community. It elevates your status and your value as you become a power person.

- All it takes to get over your fear of networking is consistent practice.

Fear is the movement from certainty to uncertainty.
—KRISHNAMURTY

I hope I have motivated you to begin building your network right away. Remember, whatever it is that you desire, focus your attention and thought on it, expect and allow yourself to achieve it, and you will, especially if you have your powerful network behind you! I wish you a life filled with abundance!

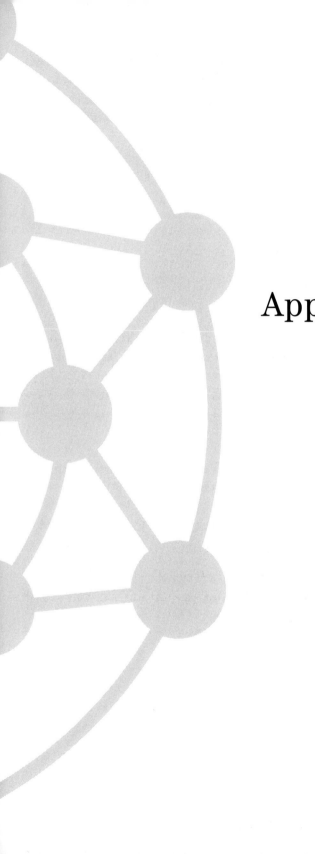

Appendix

Networking Do's and Don'ts

Here is a convenient checklist that you can use for quick review before a networking event:

DO
- Dress for the part (approachability/authority).
- Showcase your good manners.
- Respond to "Thank you" with "You're welcome" or "My pleasure" (not with "No problem!").
- Turn off the cell phone.
- Exude confidence!
- Smile and be friendly.
- Shake hands firmly.
- Circulate and decide who to approach.
- Be attentive. Apply 80/20 rule.
- Use your Company Position Statement.
- Exchange business cards.
- Make business and personal contacts.
- Recommend others. Always be helpful!
- Ask for help (people like to help—it makes them feel good).
- Keep in touch with your clients and those in your network (at least once every two months).
- Limit your time with each contact.
- Use business cards to build your network.

DON'T

- Attend in casual or business casual attire.

- Use jargon or slang.

- Attend events with friends.

- Stick with your business associates—split up and work the room from opposite ends.

- Do all the talking.

- Be loud.

- Hustle.

- Take your attention (eyes) away from the contact.

- Interrupt.

- Act bored or disinterested.

- Spend too much time with one person.

Resources

Companies that want to sell to women-owned and culturally diverse businesses may consider getting involved with these organizations:

- National Association of Women Business Owners: www.nawbo.org. NAWBO is a national organization for business women with many local chapters. Depending on the chapter, you may find start-ups and entrepreneurs to larger organizations owned and operated by women.

- National Association of Female Executives: www.nafe.org

- Women in Technology: www.WIT.org. This is also a national organization with local chapters. If you are in technology or interested in selling to this industry, attend some of their functions to determine whether it's a good fit. By the way, men are welcome to attend functions of any women's organization, so if I were a man, I'd attend these functions. Use your gender as your differentiator to get noticed quickly!

- Diversity Business: DiversityBusiness.com. This online site and magazine lists all member companies. If you're interested in doing business with diversity oriented companies, this is a good organization to join. Its also valuable if you're interested in working for a culturally diverse company.

Here are a few other national and international professional organizations for you to consider:

- Toastmasters International: www.toastmasters.org

- The Innovative Ecosystem: www.TiE.org. This group brings together startups and venture capitalists primarily in the technology and telecom industries.

- American Society for Training and Development: www.ASTD.org. ASTD is the world's largest association dedicated to workplace learning and performance professionals. Members come from more than 100 countries.

- Project Management Institute: www.pmi.org. With more than 240,000 members in over 160 countries, PMI is the leading membership association for the project management profession.

- American Marketing Association: www.ama.org.

- Mortgage Bankers Association: www.mba.org. If you're interested in selling to the financial sector, attend some MBA events to determine whether this is the right fit for you.

- American Bar Association: www.abanet.org.

- Society of CPAs. If you want to sell to this group or are a CPA and want to find a local chapter, Google "Society of CPAs" by state.

If you want to sell to federal- and state-sponsored agencies (many functions are free!):

- AFCEA: a non-profit organization that connects the government sector to the technology sector. Visit www.afcea.org.

- Small Business Development Centers. To find an SBDC in your county, do an online search for your county.

- Local chambers of commerce. Find out which ones are really active. Some are much better than others. Then get on a committee to become known quickly.

- Women's business centers (usually state funded). Do an online search for one in your area. These are very helpful organizations that offer many free services to business startups.

Index

business cards and, 32-33
company position statement and, 34
logo and, 31-32
website and, 32
Costs, of networking functions, 42-43
Country clubs, as networking venues, 49
Courtesy, 13-14, 15, 21
Credibility, 57, 59, 76, 83
Cultural diversity, 86, 142

D

Derrick, John, 135
DeWitt, Tom and Cindy, 134
Dialogue, 82-91
    80/20 rule for, 84, 93
    business card use during, 85-87
    concern for others first in, 84-85
    disengaging from (*See* Disengaging)
    at formal events, 90
    making a lasting impression during, 90-91
    mirroring during, 83
    versus monologue, 11, 12, 44
    starting, 82-83
    synchronization of styles in, 83-84
    talking about yourself during, 85
Disengaging, from dialogue, 87-88, 93
    "don't want to prevent you" method of, 88
    at formal events, 90
    turnover method of, 87-88
Diversity Business, 28, 132-133, 142
"Don't want to prevent you" method, of
    disengaging from dialogue, 87-88
Dress, appropriate, for networking events, 59-66.
    See also Personal appearance
Drinking, at networking events, 74-75
Drummond, Angela, 132-133

E

E-mail, for follow-up, 102, 103
Eating, at networking events, 73, 74
80/20 rule, 84, 93
Electronic storage, of business cards, 108-109
Elevator pitch, 11
Employees, corporate
    importance of networking for, 8
    networking strategy for, 30
    training of, 14-15
Entrepreneurs
    importance of networking for, 7
    networking strategy for, 29-30
Evaluation, of networking performance, 99-102,
    100*f*
Exchange services, and RONI, 122-123, 125
Executives, C-level. *See* C-level executives
Eye contact, 79, 83, 84
eZines, 119

F

Firing, of business provider-partners, 15
First impressions, 60, 92
Follow-up. *See* Networking follow-up

Food, at networking events, 73, 74
Formal events, networking at, 88-90
Friends
    bringing to events, 70-71, 75-76
    networking with, 48, 49

G

Global/international business, 115-118, 124
Goals
    annual revenue, 40
    for networking, 4, 35-41, 68-69, 85, 94
Graphic designers
    and business card design, 32
    as business provider-partners, 14
Greeting, at networking events, 78-81
Grooming. *See* Personal appearance
Guests, bringing to networking events, 70-71,
    75-76

H

Hair style, 62, 63, 65
Handshake, 79-81
Home court advantage, 47-48, 103
Horizontal market, 29

I

Impressions
    first, 60, 92
    lasting, 19, 90-91, 92, 119
Industry associations, as networking venues, 45
International/global business, 115-118, 124
Introduction, of self, 82-83

J

Job seekers
    importance of networking for, 7-8
    networking strategy for, 28-29
    re-entering the workforce, 134-135

K

Kenan-Flagler Business School, University of
    North Carolina, 37

L

Lead exchange, 45-46
Lead generation, 36
LinkedIn, 116-117
Logo, and corporate identity, 31-32
Loyalty, client, 8, 15, 109

M

Manners, 13-14, 15, 21, 69-70
Market
    horizontal, 29
    vertical, 28
Market segments, targeting of, 42-52
Marketing, and corporate identity, 31-34
Marketing firms, as business provider-partners, 14
Men
    handshake of, 80-81
    personal appearance of, 61, 65
Mentors, 21-22, 137

Project Management Institute (PMI), 143
Prospect(s)
    definition of, 36, 41
    member organizations of, as networking
        venues, 29-30, 46-47, 49-50
    and sales quotas, 39-41
    staying connected to, 118-120, 124
    turning suspects into, 36-37
Prospecting, 7, 36
Provider-partners. *See* Business provider-partners
Public speaking, 49-50

Q

Quotas, sales, 39-41

R

Rating system, for business cards, 97-98
Referral fees, 121
Referral sharing organizations/associations, as
    networking venues, 45-46
Relationship building, 5, 118, 122
Respect, 13-14, 15, 21
Return on Networking Investment (RONI), 101,
    107, 113-125, 131
    exchange services and, 122-123
    maximizing, 115-125
    online contact systems and, 116-118
    provider-partner relationships and, 122
    relationship building and, 118
    staying connected and, 118-120
    teaming alliances and, 121-122
    virtual sales teams and, 120-121
Revenue goals, annual, setting of, 40
RONI. *See* Return on Networking Investment
    (RONI)

S

Sales
    effectiveness of, 37-39, 38f
    monologue versus dialogue in, 44
    quotas in, 39-41
Sales teams, virtual, 43, 98, 120-121, 124-215
Sales terminology. *See* Terminology
Savar & Associates, Company Position
    Statement of, 34
Scanner, for business cards, 108
Senior executives. *See* C-level executives
Shyness, 76, 83, 104-105
SiloSmashers, 132-133
Small Business Development Centers, 144
Small business owners, importance of
    networking for, 7
Smiling, 68, 78-79, 83, 84, 104-105
SNVC, 134
Society of CPA's, 143
Soft skills, 57
Startups, networking strategy for, 29-30
Storage, of business cards, 106-111
    electronic, 108-109
    physical, 106-107

Strategic selling, 39-41
Strategy. *See* Networking strategy
Suspects, definition of, 36-37
Synchronization, of dialogue styles, 83-84
Systems architectural firms, as business
    provider-partners, 14

T

Talking, speed of, 83-84
Target market, 29-30, 42-52
Teaming alliances, 98, 121-122, 125
Technology, and etiquette, 69-70
Telemarketing, 36, 39
Terminology
    basics of, 35-37
    "business provider-partner," 12-14
    "company position statement," 12
    "elevator pitch," 11
    outdated, 10
    "vendor," 12
The Innovative Ecosystem (TiE), 143
Toastmasters International, 49-50, 143
Training firms, as business provider-partners,
    14-15
Turnover method, of disengaging from
    dialogue, 87-88

U

the Unemployed
    importance of networking for, 7-8
    networking strategy for, 28-29
United Way, 51, 89, 135
University of North Carolina, Kenan-Flagler
    Business School of, 37

V

Vendor(s)
    differences from business provider-partners,
        13-15
    as outdated terminology, 12
Venues. *See* Networking venues
Vertical market, 28
Virtual sales teams, 43, 98, 120-121, 124-215
Vista Print, 33
Voice, tone and pitch of, 83, 84
Volunteerism, 51-52. *See also* Community service

W

Warm introduction, 37
Warm leads, 121
Website, and corporate identity, 32
Women
    discrimination against, 80
    handshake of, 80-81
    networking resources for, 142
    personal appearance of, 61-66
Women in Technology, 142
Women's business centers, 144
Workforce, re-entering, 134-135

About the Author

Sheila Savar is founder and president of Savar & Associates, a firm established in 2002 to provide relationship-centric business solutions in her core areas of expertise: leadership & professional development, sales and customer care. The firm trains its culturally diverse clientele on how to provide *exceptional customer experiences* that earn client loyalty, gain and expand business opportunity and increase profitability.

Before starting her own business, Sheila enjoyed a highly successful twenty-year career in sales, customer care and senior management, primarily in the information technology industry, working for companies from fast growth start-up ventures to the Fortune 100. Clients ranged from industries such as business, technology, finance, hospitality, healthcare, manufacturing and more.

Sheila is a transformational speaker and trainer who combines her uplifting and motivational style with interactive and information-rich presentations that energize audiences into action. She is a much-in-demand international speaker and keynotes at such notable locations as The World Bank, Microsoft, AOL, BT Americas, Freddie Mac, State Farm, The Tower Club, Mortgage Bankers Association, Society of Human Resource Managers, Project Management Institute, Virginia International University and many more. She has tremendous respect from business leaders. Sheila chose networking as the topic of her first book because it is among her most requested presentation topics.

For more information, or to have Ms. Savar speak at your upcoming event or conference, please visit her website at www.savar.biz.